The
Wiersbe
BIBLE STUDY SERIES

DEUTERONOMY

The
Wiersbe
BIBLE STUDY SERIES

Acquiring

the Tools for

Spiritual

Success

David C Cook®
transforming lives together

THE WIERSBE BIBLE STUDY SERIES: DEUTERONOMY
Published by David C Cook
4050 Lee Vance View
Colorado Springs, CO 80918 U.S.A.

David C Cook Distribution Canada
55 Woodslee Avenue, Paris, Ontario, Canada N3L 3E5

David C Cook U.K., Kingsway Communications
Eastbourne, East Sussex BN23 6NT, England

The graphic circle C logo is a registered trademark of David C Cook.

All excerpts taken from *Be Equipped*, second edition, published by David C
Cook in 2010 © 1999 Warren W. Wiersbe, ISBN 978-1-4347-0052-0.

ISBN 978-0-7814-1041-0
eISBN 978-0-7814-1325-1

The Team: Steve Parolini, Karen Lee-Thorp, Amy Konyndyk, Nick
Lee, Jack Campbell, Channing Brooks, Karen Athen
Series Cover Design: John Hamilton Design

Cover Photo: iStock

Printed in the United States of America

First Edition 2015

1 2 3 4 5 6 7 8 9 10

042515

Contents

Introduction to Deuteronomy

More Than "Farewell"

The book of Deuteronomy may well be the longest farewell speech in recorded history. It's certainly the longest farewell speech found in Scripture. But it's much more than that, because in this series of addresses, Moses sought to equip this younger generation for a new life in the Promised Land. One of the most important responsibilities of the older generation is teaching the younger generation the Word of God and the principles of godly living, and Moses fulfilled that task superbly. We have the same responsibility today (2 Tim. 2:2; Titus 2:1–8), and God calls us to be faithful (1 Cor. 4:2).

The Covenant

If the Israelites obeyed God's covenant, God would bless them abundantly and the nation would be a witness to the pagan nations around them. These peoples would then want to know the God of Israel, and the Jews could explain their faith to them. Moses urged his people to love the Lord, because love is the greatest motive for obedience. So important was the book of Deuteronomy to the Jewish nation that God commanded it to be read publicly during the Feast of Tabernacles at the close of each sabbatical year (Deut. 31:10–13).

But does Deuteronomy have a message for us today? Three facts would indicate that it does: (1) All Scripture is inspired and profitable, and that includes Deuteronomy; (2) Deuteronomy is quoted in the New Testament nearly one hundred times; and (3) Jesus quoted more from Deuteronomy than from any other Old Testament book. It was the book He used when Satan tempted Him (Matt. 4:1–11) and when His enemies questioned Him (22:34–40).

The church today needs to return to the principles of godly living explained in Deuteronomy. Only then can we move forward in victory, by faith in Christ, and claim the inheritance He has appointed for us.

—*Warren W. Wiersbe*

How to Use This Study

This study is designed for both individual and small-group use. We've divided it into eight lessons—each references one or more chapters in Warren W. Wiersbe's commentary *Be Equipped* (second edition, David C Cook, 2010). While reading *Be Equipped* is not a prerequisite for going through this study, the additional insights and background Wiersbe offers can greatly enhance your study experience.

The **Getting Started** questions at the beginning of each lesson offer you an opportunity to record your first thoughts and reactions to the study text. This is an important step in the study process as those "first impressions" often include clues about what it is your heart is longing to discover.

The bulk of the study is found in the **Going Deeper** questions. These dive into the Bible text and, along with helpful excerpts from Wiersbe's commentary, help you examine not only the original context and meaning of the verses but also modern application.

Looking Inward narrows the focus down to your personal story. These intimate questions can be a bit uncomfortable at times, but don't shy away from honesty here. This is where you are asked to stand before the mirror of God's Word and look closely at what you see. It's the place to take a good look at yourself in light of the lesson and search for ways in which you can grow in faith.

Going Forward is the place where you can commit to paper those things you want or need to do in order to better live out the discoveries you made in the Looking Inward section. Don't skip or skim through this. Take the time to really consider what practical steps you might take to move closer to Christ. Then share your thoughts with a trusted friend who can act as an encourager and accountability partner.

Finally, there is a brief **Seeking Help** section to close the lesson. This is a reminder for you to invite God into your spiritual-growth process. If you choose to write out a prayer in this section, come back to it as you work through the lesson and continue to seek the Holy Spirit's guidance as you discover God's will for your life.

Tips for Small Groups

A small group is a dynamic thing. One week it might seem like a group of close-knit friends. The next it might seem more like a group of uncomfortable strangers. A small-group leader's role is to read these subtle changes and adjust the tone of the discussion accordingly.

Small groups need to be safe places for people to talk openly. It is through shared wrestling with difficult life issues that some of the greatest personal growth is discovered. But in order for the group to feel safe, participants need to know it's okay *not* to share sometimes. Always invite honest disclosure, but never force someone to speak if he or she isn't comfortable doing so. (A savvy leader will follow up later with a group member who isn't comfortable sharing in a group setting to see if a one-on-one discussion is more appropriate.)

Have volunteers take turns reading excerpts from Scripture or from the commentary. The more each person is involved even in the mundane tasks, the more they'll feel comfortable opening up in more meaningful ways.

The leader should watch the clock and keep the discussion moving. Sometimes there may be more Going Deeper questions than your group can cover in your available time. If you've had a fruitful discussion, it's okay to move on without finishing everything. And if you think the group is getting bogged down on a question or has taken off on a tangent, you can simply say, "Let's go on to question 5." Be sure to save at least ten to fifteen minutes for the Going Forward questions.

Finally, soak your group meetings in prayer—before you begin, during as needed, and always at the end of your time together.

Catching Up
(DEUTERONOMY 1—5)

Before you begin ...
- *Pray for the Holy Spirit to reveal truth and wisdom as you go through this lesson.*
- *Read Deuteronomy 1—5. This lesson references chapters 1 and 2 in* Be Equipped. *It will be helpful for you to have your Bible and a copy of the commentary available as you work through this lesson.*

Getting Started

From the Commentary

Our journalism instructor taught us that the first paragraph of every news article had to inform the reader of the "who, what, where, when, and why" of the event being reported. Deuteronomy 1:1–5 isn't a news article, but it does just that. The people of Israel are at Kadesh-barnea in the fortieth year after their deliverance from Egypt, and their leader Moses is about to expound God's law and prepare the new generation to enter Canaan. Although

Moses himself wouldn't enter the land, he would explain to the people what they had to do to conquer the enemy, claim their promised inheritance, and live successfully in their new home to the glory of God.

God was giving His people a second chance, and Moses didn't want the new generation to fail as their fathers had failed before them. Israel should have entered Canaan thirty-eight years before (2:14), but in their unbelief they rebelled against God. The Lord condemned them to wander in the wilderness until the older generation had died, with the exception of Joshua and Caleb (Num. 13—14).

—*Be Equipped*, page 15

1. How does the statement "Those who cannot remember the past are condemned to repeat it" apply to the immediate audience for the book of Deuteronomy? Why did Moses open the book by reminding the people of their past? How does this same message apply to today's church?

More to Consider: A grasp of history is important to every generation because it gives a sense of identity. If you know who you are and where you came from, you will have an easier time discovering what you should be doing. What identity did the Jews have when Moses was speaking to them? What identity did he want for them? What identity does the modern church have? What about that identity anchors us to faith?

2. Choose one verse or phrase from Deuteronomy 1—5 that stands out to you. This could be something you're intrigued by, something that makes you uncomfortable, something that puzzles you, something that resonates with you, or just something you want to examine further. Write that here.

Going Deeper
From the Commentary

After the nation left Egypt, they marched to Mount Sinai, arriving on the fifteenth day of the third month (Ex. 19:1), and there the Lord revealed Himself in power and great glory. He delivered the law to Moses, who declared it to the people, and they accepted the terms of the covenant. The Jews left Sinai on the twentieth day of the

second month of the second year after the exodus (Num.
10:11), which means they were at Sinai not quite a year.
While the nation was camped at Sinai, the tabernacle was
constructed and the priests and Levites were set apart to
serve the Lord.

—*Be Equipped*, pages 16–17

3. Why did the Lord have the Jews tarry so long at Sinai? What was the
purpose of teaching them His law during that time? Why did God give
them the law? What did the law reveal about God? About the relationship
He wanted with His people? How did the law also prepare the way for the
coming of Israel's Messiah (See Gal. 4:1–7)?

From the Commentary

Kadesh-barnea was the gateway into the Promised Land,
but Israel failed to enter the land because of fear and
unbelief. They walked by sight and not by faith in God's
promises. "See, the LORD your God has given you the
land," Moses told them. "Go up and take possession of
it…. Do not be afraid; do not be discouraged" (Deut.

1:21 NIV). It has well been said that faith is not believing in spite of evidence—that's superstition—but obeying in spite of circumstances and consequences. How much more evidence did the people need that their God was able to defeat the enemy and give them their land? Hadn't He defeated and disgraced all the false gods of Egypt, protected Israel, and provided for them on their pilgrim journey? God's commandment is always God's enablement, and to win the victory, His people need only trust and obey.

—*Be Equipped*, pages 18–19

4. What were the fears that prevented the people from entering the Promised Land? How did they walk by sight and not by faith? What are some ways we do that in today's church? Why is it so difficult sometimes to trust God's promises?

From the Commentary

The first indication that the nation was wavering in faith was their request that Moses appoint a committee to search out the land. Israel would then know the state of the land and be better able to prepare their plan of attack. This is the approach any army would use—it's called "reconnaissance"—but Israel wasn't just "any army." They were God's army and the Lord had already done the "reconnaissance" for them. From the very beginning, God had told Moses that Canaan was a good land flowing with milk and honey, and He even gave the names of the nations living in the land (Ex. 3:7–8; see Gen. 15:18–21). Surely the people knew that the will of God would not lead them where the grace and power of God could not keep them.

—*Be Equipped*, page 19

5. Read Deuteronomy 1:22–25 and Numbers 13. Why did God give Moses permission to grant the people's request (Num. 13:1–2)? How is this an example of God accommodating Himself to our condition (See Ps. 103:13–14; Judg. 6:36–40)? What should our response be to God's accommodation?

From the Commentary

Twelve men explored the land for forty days and returned to the camp with the enthusiastic, unanimous report that everything God had said about the land was true. The report shouldn't have surprised anybody because God's Word can always be trusted.

But then ten of the spies gave their opinion that Israel wasn't able to conquer the land because the cities were protected by high walls and there were giants in the land. The minority (Joshua and Caleb) boldly affirmed that the Lord was able to give His people victory because He was greater than any enemy. Unfortunately, the nation sided with the majority and became discouraged and even more afraid. Twice Moses told them not to be afraid (Deut. 1:21, 29), but his words fell on deaf ears. Instead of the leaders singing their victory song and marching forward by faith (Num. 10:35), they and the people sat in their tents complaining, weeping, and plotting to return to Egypt. With the exception of four men—Moses, Aaron, Joshua, and Caleb (14:5–6)—the entire nation rebelled against the Lord and failed to claim the land He had promised them. The Lord could bring them out of Egypt, but He couldn't take them into Canaan!

—*Be Equipped*, page 20

6. Why did the people trust the majority opinion over God's promise? What did this say about the people's faith? What had they forgotten about God? How is this a challenge in today's church as well?

From the Commentary

> When the Jews heard God's judgment declared, they tried to undo their sin in their own way, but they only made matters worse. "We have sinned!" they said, but it was a shallow confession that really meant, "We're sorry for the consequences of our sin." It wasn't true repentance; it was only regret. Then they tried to attack some of the people in the land, but their efforts failed and God brought about a humiliating defeat (Deut. 1:41–46). After all, the Lord wasn't with them and hadn't ordered them to fight. The whole enterprise was a feeble attempt on the part of the men of Israel to accomplish in their own strength what God would have accomplished for them had they only trusted Him.
>
> —*Be Equipped*, page 21

7. Why did the Jews try to "undo" their sin? In what ways is this a familiar pattern for many people today? Why didn't the Jews' tears and repentance change God's mind? What did this say about God's heart? About His expectations of His people? What should the Jews have done?

From the Commentary

> The eminent Jewish scholar Abraham Joshua Heschel wrote, "To believe, we need God, a soul, and the Word." Another Jewish scholar, the apostle Paul, reached the same conclusion and wrote, "So then faith comes by hearing, and hearing by the word of God" (Rom. 10:17 NKJV).
>
> The God who brought creation into existence by speaking the Word (Ps. 33:6–9) has ordained that His people should live by hearing and obeying His Word.
>
> —*Be Equipped*, pages 33–34

8. What is the emphasis of Deuteronomy 4:1–2, 5? Through the Bible, how does God not only teach us what to do but also explain the truths that are the reasons for His commands? In what ways was Israel's life dependent on obedience to God's Word? Is this also true for today's believers? Explain.

More to Consider: The verb "hear" is used nearly one hundred times in the book of Deuteronomy. The traditional Jewish confession of faith (Deut. 6:4–5) is called the Shema, from the Hebrew word that means "to hear, to pay attention, to understand, to obey." What does "hearing" really mean in this context? How is this true for today's Christian too?

From the Commentary

Israel's persistent sin was idolatry and the immoral practices associated with it. While living in Egypt, the Jews got a taste of idolatry and even practiced it during their wilderness wanderings (Acts 7:42–43). When Moses was with God on Mount Sinai, the people in the camp were worshipping a golden calf (Ex. 32). Idolatry was a grievous sin because Israel had been "married" to Jehovah when the nation accepted the covenant at Mount Sinai, so their worship of idols was really adultery (Jer. 3; Hos. 1—2). It was a sin against God's love as well as a violation of God's law. The Lord finally had to send His people to Babylon to cure them of idolatry.

—*Be Equipped*, pages 35–36

9. How did the tragedy of Israel's sins at Baal Peor relate to the message about idolatry (See Deut. 4:3–4; Num. 25)? What does it mean to truly fear the Lord? How were the Jews failing at this?

From the Commentary

> God's Word is the revelation of God's wisdom, and we
> need to know and follow His wisdom if our lives are to
> please and glorify Him. The world's wisdom is foolishness
> with God (1 Cor. 3:19), and those who follow it will be
> disappointed. In the Old Testament, the word "wisdom"
> has to do with character rather than human intelligence
> and describes the right use of knowledge. "Wisdom
> means being skillful and successful in one's relation-
> ships and responsibilities, observing and following the
> Creator's principles of order in the moral universe," says
> Dr. Roy Zuck. Practicing God's wisdom means you don't
> just make a living, you make a life.
>
> —*Be Equipped*, page 37

10. Review Deuteronomy 4:5–9. Why was it so important for Israel to
know and obey God's wisdom? How would knowing God's wisdom help
them succeed in their mission? How would it help them be better witnesses
to other nations? How would it help them build godly homes?

Looking Inward

Take a moment to reflect on all that you've explored thus far in this study of Deuteronomy 1—5. Review your notes and answers and think about how each of these things matters in your life today.

> *Tips for Small Groups: To get the most out of this section, form pairs or trios and have group members take turns answering these questions. Be honest and as open as you can in this discussion, but most of all, be encouraging and supportive of others. Be sensitive to those who are going through particularly difficult times and don't press for people to speak if they're uncomfortable doing so.*

11. What are some of the lessons from your past that help you avoid repeating the same sins? Do you always learn from the past? Why or why not? Why is it so easy to repeat old patterns?

12. How do you determine when someone or something is leading you astray from God's Word? If you're comfortable doing so, share a time when you were tempted to follow the ways of your culture or the people around you instead of the teaching of God. When do you struggle most to trust God's Word?

13. What does it mean to you to fear the Lord? What does that look like in practical terms? What happens when you don't fear the Lord but rely on your own wisdom?

Going Forward

14. Think of one or two things that you have learned that you'd like to work on in the coming week. Remember that this is all about quality, not quantity. It's better to work on one specific area of life and do it well than to work on many and do poorly (or to be so overwhelmed that you simply don't try).

Do you want to take some action because of your fear of the Lord? Be specific. Go back through Deuteronomy 1—5 and put a star next to the phrase or verse that is most encouraging to you. Consider memorizing this verse.

Real-Life Application Ideas: The first part of Deuteronomy is spent remembering what God has already done. Though this doesn't prevent the Jews from making future mistakes, it's certainly a worthy practice. This week, take time to review the significant events in your own faith life when God showed up or spoke to you. Write these down, and as you do, thank God for all He has done for you thus far. Revisit this history periodically to be reminded that God has been there for you in the past and that He will be there for you tomorrow. You might want to take a small-group session just to share these stories.

Seeking Help

15. Write a prayer below (or simply pray one in silence), inviting God to work on your mind and heart in those areas you've noted in the Going Forward section. Be honest about your desires and fears.

Notes for Small Groups:

- *Look for ways to put into practice the things you wrote in the Going Forward section. Talk with other group members about your ideas and commit to being accountable to one another.*

- *During the coming week, ask the Holy Spirit to continue to reveal truth to you from what you've read and studied.*

- *Before you start the next lesson, read Deuteronomy 6—7. For more in-depth lesson preparation, read chapter 3, "The Secrets of Obedience," in* Be Equipped.

Obedience
(DEUTERONOMY 6—7)

Before you begin ...
- *Pray for the Holy Spirit to reveal truth and wisdom as you go through this lesson.*
- *Read Deuteronomy 6—7. This lesson references chapter 3 in* Be Equipped. *It will be helpful for you to have your Bible and a copy of the commentary available as you work through this lesson.*

Getting Started

From the Commentary

Moses was a wise teacher of God's truth. First he reviewed what the Lord had done for Israel (Deut. 1—4) and reminded the people of God's mercy and goodness. Then he reaffirmed the basic principles of God's law (Deut. 5—6), what we know as the Ten Commandments (10:4). In chapters 6 and 7, Moses discussed motives for obedience and explained why the people should honor God's laws. He wanted the nation's obedience to be based on spiritual principles, not just personal opinions, and to be encouraged by the right motives. Only after Moses had laid this strong foundation did he apply God's commandments to specific areas of Israel's life.

—Be Equipped, page 53

1. How did God's law apply to people individually? To the nation collectively? In what ways was it meant to help the nation live together, work together, and fight the enemy together? How would the law bring people closer to God?

2. Choose one verse or phrase from Deuteronomy 6—7 that stands out to you. This could be something you're intrigued by, something that makes you uncomfortable, something that puzzles you, something that resonates with you, or just something you want to examine further. Write that here.

More to Consider: Read Psalm 119. What does this verse reveal about what the law of God meant to Jewish people who were spiritually minded and devoted to the Lord?

Going Deeper

From the Commentary

> Moses has already emphasized God's love for Israel and the importance of Israel's love for God (Deut. 4:32–43), and he will mention this topic several times before he concludes his address. If Israel obeyed the Lord, they would conquer the enemy, possess the land, multiply in the land, and enjoy a long life in the place of God's blessing (6:1–3). At least six times in this book, Moses called Canaan "a land of milk and honey" (v. 3; 11:9; 26:9, 15; 27:3; 31:20), a phrase that describes the richness and fruitfulness of the land. Milk was a staple food and honey a luxury, so "a land of milk and honey" would provide all that the people needed. There would be adequate pastures for their flocks and herds and sufficient plants in the fields for the bees to obtain pollen.
>
> —*Be Equipped*, page 54

3. Why did the people struggle to love and obey Jehovah when He blessed them so abundantly? What role, if any, might pride have played in their reluctance to obey? How did Moses attempt to address the issue of pride?

From the Commentary

The orthodox Jewish confession of faith is called "the Shema" after the Hebrew word that means "to hear." This confession is still recited each morning and evening by devout Jews all over the world, affirming "Jehovah, our Elohim, Jehovah is one." (See Matt. 22:37–38; Mark 12:29–30; Luke 10:27.) So important is this confession that Jewish boys in orthodox homes are required to memorize it as soon as they can speak. The nations around Israel worshipped many gods and goddesses, but Israel affirmed to all that there is but one true and living God, the God of Abraham, Isaac, and Jacob.

The Hebrew word translated "one" *(echad)* can also mean "a unity" as well as "numerical oneness." It's used that way in Genesis 2:24, describing the oneness of Adam and Eve, and also in Exodus 26:6 and 11 to describe "unity" of the curtains in the tabernacle (see NIV). The word also carries the idea of "uniqueness." In contrast to the many pagan gods and goddesses, Jehovah is unique, for there is only one true God; He is God alone and not part of a pantheon; and He is a unity, which Christians interpret as leaving room for the Trinity (Matt. 28:19–20; 3:16–17).

—*Be Equipped*, pages 55–56

4. Why is the theme of God's uniqueness so important to the Jews? What happens to their confession of faith if they start treating Him as one god among many?

From Today's World

In a world where "tolerance" has become a popular theme and cultural battle cry, the belief that the Christian God is the one and only God often gets lost in the noise. And it's a tricky place for Christians to be, because there's a fine line between faith that welcomes others and faith that presents itself as unique to the point of exclusion. When Christians preach about the one true God in a nation where all beliefs are (theoretically, anyway) welcome, they can come across as arrogant and intolerant. But the gospel message is actually one of inclusivity—welcoming to all who pursue a relationship with God.

5. What are the greatest challenges of holding fast to a "one true God" theology in a land where every belief system is regarded as equally "right" according to the law? What are the greatest challenges in sharing the gospel message in a culture that celebrates tolerance?

From the Commentary

Is it possible to command somebody to love? Isn't love a mysterious thing that just appears, a wonderful emotion that's either there or it isn't there? No, not according to Scripture. In the life of the believer, love is an act of the will: We choose to relate to God and to other persons in a loving way no matter how we may feel. Christian love simply means that we treat others the way God treats us. In His love, God is kind and forgiving toward us, so we seek to be kind and forgiving toward others (Eph. 4:32). God wills the very best for us, so we desire the very best for others, even if it demands sacrifice on our part. Love isn't simply an exotic feeling; love leads to action. "God so loved … that he gave" (John 3:16). The virtues of love that are listed in 1 Corinthians 13:4–7 describe how we treat people and not just how we feel about them.

—Be Equipped, page 56

6. How is love an act of the will? In what ways are loving God, worshipping Him, and serving Him the highest privileges we can have? How are we called to love God?

From the Commentary

When we hear the Word of God and receive it into our hearts (1 Thess. 2:13), then the Holy Spirit can use the truth to transform us from within (2 Cor. 3:1–3; John 17:17). God "writes" the Word upon our hearts, and we become "living epistles" that others may read, and our lives can influence them to trust Christ. How we live is important because it backs up what we say. Moses admonished parents to discuss God's Word in the home, among the children, and to allow the Word to guide their minds and hands as they work throughout the day. The Word should even control who is permitted to go through the gate and come through the door into the house. The Jews took these commandments literally and wore portions of Scripture in little containers called phylacteries on their foreheads and left arms (Matt. 23:5). They also attached a small container of Scripture, called a mezuzah, to the front door and on every door in the house. Each occupant touched the mezuzah reverently each time he or she passed through a door (Ps. 121:8). It was a sign that the house was to be a sanctuary for the Lord and a place where the Word was loved, obeyed, and taught.

—*Be Equipped*, page 57

7. How does talking about God's Word help us to embrace it? What are some of the ways Christians today engage regularly in the study and discussion of God's Word? What are examples of the church's respect for God's Word? What are the risks of not giving God's Word proper respect and honor?

From the Commentary

> Moses was equipping the new generation to enter and
> claim the Promised Land, and he knew that Canaan
> would be a place of temptation as well as a place of tri-
> umph. For one thing, when they conquered the nations
> in Canaan, the Israelites would inherit vast wealth and
> would be tempted to forget the Lord, who had made their
> victories possible. The second temptation would be for
> Israel to compromise with the pagan nations around them
> and not maintain their separated position as the people of
> the Lord. (Moses will deal with this second temptation in
> Deut. 7:1–16.)
>
> —*Be Equipped*, page 58

8. Review Deuteronomy 6:10–25. Why is prosperity often more difficult
to handle than adversity (See Phil. 4:10–20)? How is our faith tested
and strengthened during difficult times? What are practical ways to stay
focused on God in times of prosperity and good health?

More to Consider: Moses warned the people not to tempt (test) the Lord as the older generation had done at Massah (Ex. 17:1–7). What are some of the ways people tempted or tested God? How do we do that today? Why is it wrong to tempt God?

From the Commentary

"A people dwelling alone," said the hireling prophet Balaam about Israel, "not reckoning itself among the nations" (Num. 23:9 NKJV). From the call of Abraham to the exodus from Egypt, the people of Israel were expected to be a separated people, not because they were better than any other nation but because they were different. They were God's chosen people. God commanded Abraham to leave Ur of the Chaldees and go to the land that He would show him (Gen. 11:31—12:4), and when Abraham left that land and went down to Egypt for help, God had to chasten him (vv. 10–20). Throughout her history, when Israel maintained a separated position by obeying God's laws and seeking to please Him, she succeeded in all that she did. But when she began to compromise with the other nations and to worship their gods, it led to failure and defeat.

—*Be Equipped*, page 61

9. Review Deuteronomy 7:1–16. What does separation from the world mean in Scripture? How is it different from isolation? What are the dangers of being isolated from others because of a belief system? How can one be separate from others while still being the "salt of the earth" (See Matt. 5:13–16)?

From the Commentary

The first motive Moses mentioned for Israel's obedience was love for the Lord (Deut. 6:1–9), because love is the greatest motive in life. "If you love Me, keep My commandments" (John 14:15 NKJV). The second motive is gratitude (Deut. 6:10–25), for showing gratitude is one way of expressing love. We must never forget what the Lord has done for us. The third motive is separation from sin and unto the Lord (7:1–16), for we want to live up to all that God has called us to be. He's called us to be a holy nation, a chosen people, a people to bring glory to His name, and we can't fulfill any of those honorable callings if we don't separate ourselves from what is wicked and cleave to the Lord.

But these three motives all depend on faith in the promises of God, for "without faith it is impossible to please [God]" (Heb. 11:6). Israel wasn't operating on what the world calls "blind faith" because they had God's covenant promises to encourage them and the long record of God's care to assure them. God's people don't live on explanations; they live on promises. At the end of his life, Joshua reminded the people, "And you know in all your hearts and in all your souls that not one thing has failed of all the good things which the LORD your God spoke concerning you" (Josh. 23:14 NKJV).

—*Be Equipped*, pages 64–65

10. How does each of the three motives mentioned in the previous commentary excerpt depend on faith in God's promises? What does it mean to live on God's promises? How does the covenant relationship influence the people's willingness and ability to trust God?

Looking Inward

Take a moment to reflect on all that you've explored thus far in this study of Deuteronomy 6—7. Review your notes and answers and think about how each of these things matters in your life today.

> *Tips for Small Groups: To get the most out of this section, form pairs or trios and have group members take turns answering these questions. Be honest and as open as you can in this discussion, but most of all, be encouraging and supportive of others. Be sensitive to those who are going through particularly difficult times and don't press for people to speak if they're uncomfortable doing so.*

11. What does obedience mean to you? In what ways is obeying God easy for you? How is it difficult? What role does the Holy Spirit play in helping you to obey God?

12. What does it mean to you that God is the one true God? How does this affect the way you approach your faith? What are some of the ways the world tests your beliefs about God?

13. What does it mean to be *in* the world but not *of* it? What are some of the ways you're separate from nonbelievers? How can you be both separate and welcoming of those seeking the truth?

Going Forward

14. Think of one or two things that you have learned that you'd like to work on in the coming week. Remember that this is all about quality, not quantity. It's better to work on one specific area of life and do it well than to work on many and do poorly (or to be so overwhelmed that you simply don't try).

Do you want to take a step toward better obedience to God? Be specific. Go back through Deuteronomy 6—7 and put a star next to the phrase or verse that is most encouraging to you. Consider memorizing this verse.

Real-Life Application Ideas: This week, think about what it means to be separate because of your faith. What does that look like in practical terms? How does your relationship with God affect the way you relate to your family? To your coworkers? To strangers? What are some ways your separateness gets in the way of relationships with others? Be mindful this week of the specialness of being in relationship with God and how it can both give you peace and prompt you to reach out to others.

Seeking Help

15. Write a prayer below (or simply pray one in silence), inviting God to work on your mind and heart in those areas you've noted in the Going Forward section. Be honest about your desires and fears.

Notes for Small Groups:

- *Look for ways to put into practice the things you wrote in the Going Forward section. Talk with other group members about your ideas and commit to being accountable to one another.*

- *During the coming week, ask the Holy Spirit to continue to reveal truth to you from what you've read and studied.*

- *Before you start the next lesson, read Deuteronomy 8—11. For more in-depth lesson preparation, read chapter 4, "See What You Are," in* Be Equipped.

What Are You?
(DEUTERONOMY 8—11)

Before you begin ...
- *Pray for the Holy Spirit to reveal truth and wisdom as you go through this lesson.*
- *Read Deuteronomy 8—11. This lesson references chapter 4 in* Be Equipped. *It will be helpful for you to have your Bible and a copy of the commentary available as you work through this lesson.*

Getting Started

From the Commentary

Oliver Cromwell told the artist painting his portrait that he refused to pay even a farthing for the painting unless it truly looked like him, including "pimples, warts, and everything as you see me." Apparently the Lord Protector of the Commonwealth of England, Scotland, and Ireland was as courageous sitting for a portrait as he was leading an army on the battlefield. Most of us aren't that brave. We're uncomfortable looking at unretouched proofs of our photographs, and we'd certainly willingly pay for a painting that improved our appearance.

In this part of his farewell address, Moses painted the people of Israel as they really were, "warts and all."

—*Be Equipped*, page 73

1. What were the "warts" that Moses included in his description of the people? How are these like the warts the church has today? Why was it important for Moses to be honest in his portrayal of the people? How does that kind of honesty today help us to grow closer to Christ?

2. Choose one verse or phrase from Deuteronomy 8—11 that stands out to you. This could be something you're intrigued by, something that makes you uncomfortable, something that puzzles you, something that resonates with you, or just something you want to examine further. Write that here.

Going Deeper

From the Commentary

The three essentials for Israel's conquest and enjoyment of the Promised Land were: listening to God's Word, remembering it, and obeying it. They are still the essentials for a successful and satisfying Christian life today. As we walk through this world, we can't succeed without God's guidance, protection, and provision, and it also helps to have a good memory. Four times in these chapters Moses commands us to remember (Deut. 8:2, 18; 9:7, 27), and four more times he admonishes us to forget not (8:11, 14, 19; 9:7). The apostle Peter devoted his second letter to the ministry of reminding God's people to remember what the apostles had taught them (2 Peter 1:12–18; 3:1–2). Moses pointed out four ministries God performed for Israel and that He performs for us today as He seeks to mature us and prepare us for what He has planned for us.

The first ministry involves God testing us (Deut. 8:1–2).

—*Be Equipped*, pages 73–74

3. Review Deuteronomy 8:1–2. What does it mean to be tested by God? What were some ways He tested the Jews? How does God test us today? What is the purpose of that testing?

*More to Consider: Life is a school (Ps. 90:12), and we often don't
know what the lesson was until after we have failed the examination!
Read Jeremiah 17:9. Why can't the heart be trusted? How does our
response to testing reveal the truth in our hearts?*

From the Commentary

The second ministry involves God teaching us (Deut. 8:3).
Each morning during their wilderness journey, God sent
the Jewish people "angels' food" (Ps. 78:21–25) to teach
them to depend on Him for what they needed. But the
manna was much more than daily physical sustenance;
it was a type of the coming Messiah who is "the bread of
life" (John 6:35). When Satan tempted Him to turn stones
into bread (Matt. 4:1–4), Jesus quoted Deuteronomy 8:3
and indicated that the Word of God is also the bread of
God, for we "feed on" Jesus Christ when we "feed on"
the Word of God. God was teaching the Jews to look to
Him for "daily bread" (Matt. 6:11) and to begin each day
meditating on the Word of God.

—*Be Equipped*, pages 74–75

4. What is the "manna" that God provides for us today? What does our
relationship with that manna indicate about our relationship with God?

From Today's World

In a world where social media rules, it's common for people to curate their online lives so that they present a certain kind of image for others to see. They may post photos of their "perfect family vacation," or share only the positive highlights of their lives. Meanwhile, public figures manage their images with carefully worded press releases, and magazines present pictures of models with digitally altered, blemish-free skin. It's a world of "what you see is what we want you to see" rather than a world where transparency and truth rule.

5. Why is it so tempting to hide the blemishes in our lives from others? What are we afraid of? How does embracing the truth of our warts help us to grow in relationship with God? With others?

From the Commentary

The third ministry involves God caring for us (Deut. 8:4; 29:5). Not only did God feed the Jews "miracle bread" each morning, but He also kept their clothes from wearing out and their feet from swelling. The three pressing questions of life for most people are "What shall we eat? What shall we drink? What shall we wear?" (Matt. 6:25–34), and the Lord met all these needs for His people for forty years. "Casting all your care upon Him, for He cares for you" (1 Peter 5:7 NKJV). "For your heavenly Father knows that you need all these things" (Matt. 6:32 NKJV).

—*Be Equipped*, page 75

6. God doesn't deliver bread, water, and clothing to our front doors each day. So how does He provide for us? What does God's care look like in the church today? Why is it so important for us to recognize God's care? What happens when we don't?

From the Commentary

The fourth ministry involves God disciplining us (Deut. 8:5). God saw the children of Israel as His own children whom He greatly loved. "Israel is my son, even my first-born" (Ex. 4:22; see Hos. 11:1). After years of slavery in Egypt, the Jews had to learn what freedom was and how to use it responsibly. We commonly think of "discipline" only as punishment for disobedience, but much more is involved. Discipline is "child training," the preparation of the child for responsible adulthood. A judge justly punishes a convicted criminal in order to protect society and uphold the law, but a father lovingly disciplines a child to help that child mature. Discipline is evidence of God's love and of our membership in God's family (Heb. 12:5–8; Prov. 3:11–12).

—*Be Equipped*, pages 75–76

7. What does God's discipline of His children look like? What is the purpose of discipline? What should be our response to God's discipline (See Deut. 8:2–3; Heb. 12:9–10)? What happens to our hearts when we resist His discipline?

From the Commentary

After being set free from Egypt, Israel's destination wasn't the wilderness; it was the Promised Land, the place of their inheritance. "And he [God] brought us out from thence [Egypt] that he might bring us in" (Deut. 6:23). So with the Christian life: Being born again and redeemed from sin are only the beginning of our walk with Christ, a great beginning, to be sure, but only a beginning. If like Israel at Kadesh-barnea we rebel in unbelief, then we will wander through life and never enjoy what God planned for us (Eph. 2:10; Heb. 3—4). But if we surrender to the Lord and obey His will, He will enable us to be "more than conquerors" (Rom. 8:37) as we claim our inheritance in Christ and serve Him.

—*Be Equipped*, page 76

8. What did it mean for the Jews to be "more than conquerors" in Moses' time? What does it mean for believers today? What role does obedience play in our ability to receive our promised inheritance?

More to Consider: Moses mentioned water in Deuteronomy 8:6–9: streams, pools, and springs flowing in the hills and valleys. Later in the book he talked about God's promise to send the autumn and spring rains each year (11:14). With God's blessing, an abundance of water would make possible an abundance of crops, and the Israelites would harvest grain, grapes, figs, and olives, and they would also find honey. How does this typify the spiritual wealth believers today have in Christ (See Eph. 1:7, 18; 2:4, 7; 3:8, 16)?

From the Commentary

For the fifth time in his address, Moses says, "Hear, O Israel!" (Deut. 9:1; see also 4:1; 5:1; 6:3–4). He was giving the people the Word of God, and when God speaks to His people, they must listen. The word "hear" is used over fifty times in Deuteronomy, for God's people live by faith, and "faith cometh by hearing, and hearing by the word of God" (Rom. 10:17). The Jews couldn't see their God, but they could hear Him, while their pagan neighbors could see their gods but couldn't hear them (Ps. 115:5). In Deuteronomy 9:1—10:11, Moses reminded the people that their conduct since leaving Egypt had been anything but exemplary, in spite of His long-suffering and grace.

—*Be Equipped*, pages 78–79

9. Review Deuteronomy 9:1—10:11. What does this section teach us about the grace of God? About God's discipline? About Israel's sins? What does

it tell us about God's faithfulness? Why is this the most important lesson in this section?

From the Commentary

> "And now, Israel" (Deut. 10:12) forms a transition as Moses moves into the closing section of this part of his address, a section in which he reminds the people why they should obey the Lord their God. This was not a new topic, but it was an important topic, and Moses wanted them to get the message and not forget it: Loving obedience to the Lord is the key to every blessing. Jesus often repeated truths He had already shared, and Paul wrote to the Philippians, "For me to write the same things to you is not tedious, but for you it is safe" (Phil. 3:1 NKJV).
>
> —*Be Equipped*, page 84

10. Review Deuteronomy 10:12—11:32. Why did Moses give this message of obedience once again? How was repetition an important teaching method during Moses' time? What aids do we have today in learning and remembering God's Word that people didn't have in Moses' time?

Looking Inward

Take a moment to reflect on all that you've explored thus far in this study of Deuteronomy 8—11. Review your notes and answers and think about how each of these things matters in your life today.

Tips for Small Groups: To get the most out of this section, form pairs or trios and have group members take turns answering these questions. Be honest and as open as you can in this discussion, but most of all, be encouraging and supportive of others. Be sensitive to those who are going through particularly difficult times and don't press for people to speak if they're uncomfortable doing so.

11. What are some ways God has tested you? What did you learn through those experiences? How have you grown?

12. How has God provided for you and those you love? List some of the things God has done to send "manna" to you. How have you responded to God's provision? How has it brought you closer to God?

13. Moses used repetition to teach important messages to the people. But today we have access to myriad resources to remind us of God's truths. What are some ways you continue to study and embrace God's truth? How does repetition of God's messages help you engage with them?

Going Forward

14. Think of one or two things that you have learned that you'd like to work on in the coming week. Remember that this is all about quality, not quantity. It's better to work on one specific area of life and do it well than to work on many and do poorly (or to be so overwhelmed that you simply don't try).

Do you want to do a better job of trusting God in the midst of testing? Be specific. Go back through Deuteronomy 8—11 and put a star next to the phrase or verse that is most encouraging to you. Consider memorizing this verse.

Real-Life Application Ideas: God has provided much for you. This week, be the hands and feet of God and provide for others who are in need. Volunteer at a soup kitchen or another community service organization. Offer to help a neighbor with a project. Donate time and resources to someone in need. God's provision often comes through the efforts of His people. Be one of those people this week.

Seeking Help

15. Write a prayer below (or simply pray one in silence), inviting God to work on your mind and heart in those areas you've noted in the Going Forward section. Be honest about your desires and fears.

Notes for Small Groups:

- *Look for ways to put into practice the things you wrote in the Going Forward section. Talk with other group members about your ideas and commit to being accountable to one another.*

- *During the coming week, ask the Holy Spirit to continue to reveal truth to you from what you've read and studied.*

- *Before you start the next lesson, read Deuteronomy 12:1—16:17; 18:9–22. For more in-depth lesson preparation, read chapters 5 and 6, "Worship Him in Truth" and "Food and Festivals," in* Be Equipped.

Worship

(DEUTERONOMY 12:1—16:17; 18:9–22)

Before you begin ...

- *Pray for the Holy Spirit to reveal truth and wisdom as you go through this lesson.*
- *Read Deuteronomy 12:1—16:17; 18:9–22. This lesson references chapters 5 and 6 in* Be Equipped. *It will be helpful for you to have your Bible and a copy of the commentary available as you work through this lesson.*

Getting Started

From the Commentary

Moses was a wise instructor. He devoted the first part of his address (Deut. 1—5) to reviewing the past and helping the new generation appreciate all that God had done for them. Then he told the people how they should respond to the goodness of God and why they should obey Jehovah (Deut. 6—11). In other words, Moses was helping his people develop hearts of love for the Lord, because if they loved Him, they would obey Him. Moses repeated God's covenant promises to the nation but also balanced the promises with the warnings of what would happen if they disobeyed. More than anything else, Moses wanted the Israelites to mature in faith and love so they could enter the land, conquer the enemy, and enjoy their inheritance to the glory of God.

In Deuteronomy 12—26, Moses built on this foundation and applied the law to Israel's new situation in the Promised Land. The Jews had been slaves in Egypt and nomads in the wilderness, but now they would become conquerors and tenants in God's land (Lev. 25:23 NIV).

—*Be Equipped*, page 95

1. Why was it important that God set down the rules for the Jews now that they were about to enter the Promised Land? How could those rules help the people enjoy the land and God's blessing?

More to Consider: The statement in Deuteronomy 12:1 was both an assurance and a commandment. The assurance was that Israel would enter the land and overcome the enemy, and the commandment was that, having entered the land, they would have to purge it of all idolatry. This wasn't a new commandment, for Moses had mentioned it before (Num. 33:50–56; Deut. 7:1–6, 23–26) and he would mention it again. Why was idolatry such a dangerous temptation for the people? How is this true in today's church?

2. Choose one verse or phrase from Deuteronomy 12:1—16:17; 18:9–22 that stands out to you. This could be something you're intrigued by, something that makes you uncomfortable, something that puzzles you, something that resonates with you, or just something you want to examine further. Write that here.

Going Deeper

From the Commentary

> "You must not worship the LORD your God in their way" (Deut. 12:4 NIV) is a simple statement that carries a powerful message. As the people of God, we must worship the Lord the way He commands and not imitate the religious

practices of others. The Jewish faith and the Christian faith came by revelation, not by man's invention or Satan's instruction (1 Tim. 4:1; 2 Tim. 3:5–7). The most important activity of the church is the worship of God because everything truly spiritual that the church does flows out of worship.

—*Be Equipped*, page 97

3. What are some "wrong" ways to worship God? Why are they wrong? What does true worship look like? What does the way a person worships reveal about his or her relationship with God? What does the way a church worships say about that church?

From the Commentary

Canaanite worship permitted the people to offer whatever sacrifices they pleased at whatever place they chose, but for Israel there was to be but one altar. The Jews were allowed to kill and eat livestock and wild game at any place (Deut. 12:15, 21–22), but these animals were not to be offered as sacrifices when they were killed. The only place where sacrifices were accepted was at the altar of God's sanctuary, and the only people who could offer them were the Lord's appointed priests. The Lord didn't want His people inventing their own religious system by imitating the practices of the pagan nations. During the decadent days of the judges, that's exactly what some of the people did (Judg. 17—18).

—*Be Equipped*, page 99

4. Review Deuteronomy 12:6–7, 12–14. What was significant about having a single altar? What did the burnt offerings symbolize (See Lev. 1)? How is Paul's message in Romans 12:1–2 similar to what the burnt offerings symbolized?

From the Commentary

Deuteronomy 12:15–16, 20–28 focuses on the Jews' treatment of the blood of animals that were either sacrificed at the altar or eaten at home, a theme Moses discussed in Leviticus 17:1–16. The Lord introduced this theme after Noah and his family came out of the ark, for

it was then that He permitted mankind to eat meat (Gen.
9:1–7; and see 1:29; 2:9, 16). In the Genesis legislation,
God prohibited the shedding of human blood and the
eating of animal blood, whether the animal was domestic
or wild. He also established what we today call "capital
punishment." Since humans are made in the image of
God and derive their life from God, to murder someone
is to attack God and to rob that person of God's gift of
life. God decreed that murderers should be punished by
losing their own lives, and the right to enforce this law
belonged to the officers of the state (Rom. 13).

—*Be Equipped*, page 100

5. What do the laws about respecting life teach us about the nature of God?
About God's plan for His people? About the value of each human life?

From the Commentary

The practice of bringing 10 percent of the produce to
the Lord antedates the law, for Abraham tithed (Gen.
14:17–20; Heb. 7:4) and so did Jacob (Gen. 28:22). In

most places in the world today, God's people bring money rather than produce. The New Testament plan for giving is found in 2 Corinthians 8—9, and though tithing isn't mentioned, generous giving from the heart is encouraged. If believers under law could give the Lord 10 percent of their income, that's certainly a good place for believers who live under the new covenant to start their giving. However, we shouldn't stop with 10 percent but should give systematically as the Lord has prospered us (1 Cor. 16:1–2).

The priests and Levites had no inheritance in the land of Israel, for the Lord was their inheritance (Num. 18:20; Deut. 10:8–9; Josh. 13:14, 33; 14:13; 18:7), so they trusted God for His provision through the people. God assigned to the priests portions from various sacrifices (Lev. 6:14—7:38) as well as the firstfruits of the harvests and the firstborn animals (Num. 18:8–20). The Levites received the people's tithes and in turn gave a tithe of that to the priests (vv. 20–32). The people also brought an extra tithe every three years, which was shared with the poor. People who lived too far from the sanctuary were permitted to sell the produce and with the money buy a substitute sacrifice when they arrived (Deut. 14:24–26), and if they didn't do so, they were fined.

—Be Equipped, pages 101–2

6. Read Luke 10:7 and 1 Corinthians 9:14. What do these verses tell us about the responsibility of the people to their leaders? Why is the idea of

giving tithes and offerings often a controversial one in churches? What is the core purpose of offerings? How can that purpose be misconstrued or manipulated? What are practical ways to assure the church is approaching the concept of tithes and offerings from a biblical perspective?

From the Commentary

> Moses pointed out four approaches the Enemy could use to trap the Israelites into practicing idolatry, and he warned his people to avoid following them.
>
> (1) Human curiosity (Deut. 12:29–32).
>
> (2) Temptation from the prophets (Deut. 13:1–5).
>
> (3) Temptation from friends and relatives (Deut. 13:6–11).
>
> (4) Temptation from a multitude (Deut. 13:12–18).
>
> —*Be Equipped*, pages 102–6

7. Review all four approaches mentioned in the previous commentary excerpt. How is each of these a trap that could lead to idolatry? Why would Moses need to warn the people about these traps? Wouldn't they already

know about these temptations? How are these traps similar for today's believers?

From the Commentary

> We must never take for granted that we are "the children of the LORD [our] God" and "a holy people to the LORD [our] God" (Deut. 14:1–2 NKJV). These are privileges that we don't deserve and that we could never earn, and we enjoy them only because of God's love and grace. The Lord announced to Pharaoh, "Israel is my son, even my firstborn" (Ex. 4:22; see Jer. 31:9), and because Pharaoh wouldn't listen and obey, Egypt lost all their firstborn.
>
> At Sinai, before He gave the law, the Lord announced to Israel, "And you shall be to Me a kingdom of priests and a holy nation" (Ex. 19:6 NKJV). Because of their unique relationship to the Lord as His chosen people and special treasure, the Israelites were responsible to obey Him and truly be a holy people. Their relationship to the Lord was the most important factor in their national life, for without the Lord, Israel would be like all the other nations.
>
> —*Be Equipped*, pages 117–18

8. What does it mean to be a holy people? What are the responsibilities that accompany holiness? How do the verses in Deuteronomy 14 address the concept of holiness? Does holiness today look different than it did in Moses' time? Explain.

More to Consider: The distinction between clean and unclean sacrifices was known in the days of Noah (Gen. 7:1–10) and therefore must have been told to the following generation when God taught them to worship. In the Jewish law, the words "clean" and "unclean" have nothing to do with the intrinsic nature or value of the creatures themselves. This was a designation given by the Lord for reasons not always explained. How has our understanding of these words changed over time? Read 1 Corinthians 8:8 and Colossians 2:16–23. What do these verses teach us about the relationship between what we eat and our spirituality?

From the Commentary

When we studied Deuteronomy 12, we learned that God commanded His people to give 10 percent of their produce (grain, fruits, vegetables, and animals) to Him as an act of worship and an expression of gratitude for His blessing. Every year, each family had to go to the sanctuary with their tithes, enjoy a feast there, and share the tithe with the Levites, who, in turn, would share it with the priests (Num. 18:20–32). Moses repeated this commandment, because when it comes to giving to the Lord, some people need more than one reminder (2 Cor. 8:10–11; 9:1–5).

The people of Israel were to be generous with tithes and offerings because the Lord had been generous with them. Each time they brought their tithes and gifts to the sanctuary and enjoyed a thanksgiving feast, it would teach them to fear the Lord (Deut. 14:23), because if the Lord hadn't blessed them, they would have nothing to eat and nothing to give.

—*Be Equipped*, page 121

9. Read 1 Chronicles 29:16. What does David's message teach us about that which we give to God? What happens to our generosity when we fail to appreciate God's bountiful provision?

From the Commentary

> Those who think that it takes a great deal of faith to give
> God a tithe of their income will probably be shocked when
> they read Deuteronomy 15:1–18. Just as every seventh day
> of the week was set apart for God as the Sabbath Day, so
> every seventh year was to be set apart as a Sabbath Year.
> During that year, the Jews were not to cultivate the land
> but allow it to rest. The people would have to trust God
> to produce the grain, vegetables, and fruits they needed
> for themselves and for their flocks and herds and farm
> animals. (See Lev. 25:1–7.) Every fiftieth year was a "Year
> of Jubilee" (v. 8ff.) when the land lay fallow for another
> year! It would really take faith on the part of the people to
> trust God for what they needed for two long years!
>
> —*Be Equipped*, page 122

10. Is there any parallel in today's church to the Sabbath Year or the Year
of Jubilee? Why or why not? What are the biggest tests of faith that today's
church experiences? In what ways do we trust God for our needs today?

Looking Inward

Take a moment to reflect on all that you've explored thus far in this study of Deuteronomy 12:1—16:17; 18:9–22. Review your notes and answers and think about how each of these things matters in your life today.

Tips for Small Groups: To get the most out of this section, form pairs or trios and have group members take turns answering these questions. Be honest and as open as you can in this discussion, but most of all, be encouraging and supportive of others. Be sensitive to those who are going through particularly difficult times and don't press for people to speak if they're uncomfortable doing so.

11. How comfortable are you with following rules? What would have been your greatest challenge if you'd lived in Moses' time? How do you reconcile the Old Testament law with the law of grace that Jesus introduced with His life, death, and resurrection?

12. How do you best worship? What does worship do for you? How does it bring you closer to God? What happens to your relationship with God when you neglect worship?

13. What does holiness mean to you? Do you consider yourself a holy person? Explain. How can you pursue holiness without it becoming self-serving or all about your image?

Going Forward

14. Think of one or two things that you have learned that you'd like to work on in the coming week. Remember that this is all about quality, not quantity. It's better to work on one specific area of life and do it well than to work on many and do poorly (or to be so overwhelmed that you simply don't try).

Do you want to live a holier life? Be specific. Go back through Deuteronomy 12:1—16:17; 18:9–22 and put a star next to the phrase or verse that is most encouraging to you. Consider memorizing this verse.

Real-Life Application Ideas: This week, take time out of each day to focus on worshipping God. You can do this in a number of ways— through singing, studying, prayer, fellowship, serving. As you worship God, pay special attention to how worshipping brings you closer to Him and what worshipping teaches you about humility, honor, and praise. Then consider adding more intentional worship times to your weekly routine—don't just wait for Sunday to worship God.

Seeking Help

15. Write a prayer below (or simply pray one in silence), inviting God to work on your mind and heart in those areas you've noted in the Going Forward section. Be honest about your desires and fears.

Notes for Small Groups:

- *Look for ways to put into practice the things you wrote in the Going Forward section. Talk with other group members about your ideas and commit to being accountable to one another.*

- *During the coming week, ask the Holy Spirit to continue to reveal truth to you from what you've read and studied.*

- *Before you start the next lesson, read Deuteronomy 16:18—18:8; 19:1—21:14; 26:1–19. For more in-depth lesson preparation, read chapters 7 and 8, "Judges, Kings, Priests, and Ordinary People" and "Manslaughter, War, and Murder," in* Be Equipped.

All Kinds of People

(DEUTERONOMY 16:18—18:8; 19:1—21:14; 26:1–19)

Before you begin ...
- *Pray for the Holy Spirit to reveal truth and wisdom as you go through this lesson.*
- *Read Deuteronomy 16:18—18:8; 19:1—21:14; 26:1–19. This lesson references chapters 7 and 8 in* Be Equipped. *It will be helpful for you to have your Bible and a copy of the commentary available as you work through this lesson.*

Getting Started

From the Commentary

As Moses continued to prepare the new generation for life in the Promised Land, he not only instructed them about their past history and their obligations in worship, but he also explained to them the kind of government God wanted them to organize. When their ancestors were in Egypt, the Jews had minimal organization involving only elders (Ex. 3:18), and during the wilderness journey,

Moses had tribal officers who assisted him in solving the problems the people brought them (18:13ff.). Each tribe in Israel also had a leader (Num. 1:5–16; 7:10–83), and there were seventy elders who assisted Moses in the spiritual oversight of the nation (11:10ff.).

This basic organization was adequate to govern a nomadic people following a gifted leader, but it wouldn't suffice once the nation moved into the Promised Land. For one thing, Moses would no longer be with them to give them messages directly from the mouth of God. Furthermore, each of the twelve tribes would be living in its own assigned territory, and Reuben, Gad, and Manasseh would be located on the other side of the Jordan River. How would they deal with tribal differences? Who would protect the people and enforce God's laws? God in His grace gave them the kind of government that would meet their needs.

—*Be Equipped*, pages 135–36

1. What were the basic offices and obligations of the government, according to Moses? Why was it so important to define these roles? How does this keep people accountable? How does it provide a foundation for pursuing a relationship with God? What implications concerning authority does this message have for us today?

2. Choose one verse or phrase from Deuteronomy 16:18—18:8; 19:1—21:14; 26:1–19 that stands out to you. This could be something you're intrigued by, something that makes you uncomfortable, something that puzzles you, something that resonates with you, or just something you want to examine further. Write that here.

Going Deeper

From the Commentary

> The most important thing about the judges and officers was that they be men of character, because only just men could honestly execute just judgment. The judges were not to twist the law and "distort justice," nor were they to "respect persons," which in the Hebrew is literally "regard faces." The important thing was to determine what the accused person did and not to major on who the accused person was. The Lord warned the judges not to favor their friends by acquitting the guilty, reducing the sentences, or tampering with the legal process, nor were the judges to accept bribes. "Justice" is usually pictured as a woman carrying scales and wearing a blindfold. "It is not good

to show partiality to the wicked, or to overthrow the righteous in judgment" (Prov. 18:5 NKJV).

The decisions of the judges affected not only the individuals on trial but the entire nation.

—*Be Equipped*, page 137

3. Review Deuteronomy 16:19–20. What is the definition of a person having character? Why was good character critically important for judges? How does that match up with the character of today's leaders? What are the dangers of having someone with questionable character in charge? What role does a person's faith play in determining his or her character?

More to Consider: What types of people are cut out for leadership in the church (See Acts 6:1–7; 1 Tim. 3; Titus 1:5–9)? What are the best ways to determine who's qualified for leadership? How do you deal with leaders who exercise questionable judgment?

From the Commentary

Idolatry was the great enemy of the spiritual life of the Jewish nation, and the judges had to be alert enough to detect it and courageous enough to deal with it. The "groves" were areas dedicated to the worship of Baal's consort, Ashtoreth, and among their idols were wooden poles that symbolized the male member. Note that the idolaters tried to locate their worship centers as close to God's altar as possible (Deut. 16:21; NIV, "beside the altar"). The idolaters wanted to encourage people to worship both Jehovah and Ashtoreth, and eventually Ashtoreth would win out. If the judges were devoted to God, they would carefully investigate such practices, get the facts, condemn the guilty, and remove the idols from the land. They had to put Jehovah first.

It can't be emphasized too much that the religion of the Canaanite nations was unspeakably filthy and mingled blind superstition with gross immorality.

—Be Equipped, page 138

4. Review Deuteronomy 16:21—17:7. Why did God command the Jews to wipe out every vestige of Canaanite religion from the land (See 7:1–11)? What does this say about human nature? What does it say about God?

From the Commentary

Elected leaders, not hereditary rulers, govern democratic nations today, but in ancient times, kings and emperors ruled nations and empires with despotic authority. But Israel was different from the other nations, for the law of the Lord was the "cement" that united the twelve tribes. The Levites, who were scattered throughout the land, taught the people God's law, and the priests and judges saw to it that the law was enforced justly. The Israelites had to bring their tithes and sacrifices to the central sanctuary, and three times each year all the adult males assembled there to celebrate the goodness of the Lord. Jehovah was King in Israel (Ex. 15:18; Judg. 8:23) and He sat "enthroned between the cherubim" (Ps. 80:1 NIV) in the Holy of Holies.

But the Lord knew that the day would come when Israel would ask for a king because they wanted to be like the other nations (1 Sam. 8). During the time of the judges, the political and spiritual unity of the twelve tribes deteriorated greatly (Judg. 17:6; 21:25), and Israel was in constant danger of invasion by their enemies (1 Sam. 9:16; 12:12). Instead of trusting God, the people wanted a king who would build an army and lead the nation to victory. Unfortunately, the spiritual leadership in Israel had decayed, and Samuel's sons weren't following the ways of the Lord (8:1–5). But the main cause for Israel's cry for a king was their desire to be like the other nations. Yet Israel's great distinction was that they were not like the other nations! They were God's chosen people, a kingdom of priests, and God's special treasure (Ex. 19:5–6). "Lo, the people shall dwell alone, and shall not be reckoned among the nations" (Num. 23:9).

—*Be Equipped*, pages 139–40

5. Why is imitating the world instead of trusting the Lord such a great temptation for God's people? How is this true in today's church? What is the inevitable result of trusting other people instead of God?

From the Commentary

The church of Jesus Christ *is* a priesthood (1 Peter 2:5, 9), but the nation of Israel *had* a priesthood. All the priests and Levites were descendants of Levi, Jacob's third son by Leah. Levi had three sons—Gershon, Kohath, and Merari—and Aaron and Moses were from the family of Kohath (Ex. 6:16–25). Only the descendants of Aaron were called "priests" and were allowed to serve at the altar and in the sanctuary proper. The Levites, who were descendants of Gershon and Merari, assisted the priests in the many ministries connected with the altar and the sanctuary. Neither the priests nor the Levites were given any inheritance in the land of Israel (Deut. 10:8–9; 12:12, 18–19) but lived from the tithes, offerings, and sacrifices that were brought to the sanctuary.

The priests were to receive specified parts from the sacrifices, except for the burnt offering, which was totally consumed on the altar. They would burn a handful of the meal offering on the altar and keep the rest for themselves, and various parts of the animal sacrifices were given to them as their due (Lev. 6:8—7:38). They were also given the firstfruits of the grain, oil, wine, and wool.

—*Be Equipped*, page 142

6. What was the symbolic significance of the firstfruits? Read 1 Corinthians 9:13–14. How does this New Testament passage relate to the Old Testament practice described in the previous commentary excerpt?

From the Commentary

> It isn't enough for a nation to have gifted and godly lead-
> ers; it must also have godly citizens who obey the law of
> the Lord. Confucius said, "The strength of a nation is
> derived from the integrity of its homes." But homes are
> made up of individuals, so it's the strength of the indi-
> vidual that helps to make the home what it ought to be.
> "Whatever makes men good Christians," said Daniel
> Webster, "makes them good citizens."
>
> —*Be Equipped*, pages 143–44

7. The three confessions described in Deuteronomy 26 are the confession
of God's goodness (vv. 1–11), the confession of honesty and generosity
(vv. 12–15), and the confession of obedience (vv. 16–19). What does each
of them teach us about what kind of citizens we ought to be as followers
of Christ?

From the Commentary

The Quaker poet John Greenleaf Whittier called justice "the hope of all who suffer, the dread of all who wrong." That's the ideal, but it isn't always achieved in real life. Without justice, society would fall apart, anarchy would take over, and it wouldn't be safe for people to leave their homes. Israel didn't have the elaborate police system we have today, so locating and punishing guilty criminals depended primarily on the elders and the judges. By singling out the "cities of refuge," the Lord promoted justice in the land.

In Deuteronomy 19:1–3, 7–10, Moses reviews what he had taught Israel in Numbers 35; in fact, he had already set up the three cities of refuge east of the Jordan (Deut. 4:42–43). It would be Joshua's responsibility to set up the other three cities west of the Jordan after Israel had conquered the land (Josh. 20). Those east of the Jordan were Golan, Ramoth, and Bezer, and on the west, they would be Kedesh, Shechem, and Hebron. If you consult a map of the Holy Land, you will see that these cities were so located that they were easily accessible to those who needed protection. The roads leading to these cities were to be kept in good repair and be clearly marked. Rabbinical tradition states that there were signs at all the crossroads pointing the way to the nearest city of refuge. The Lord wanted to make it easy for the innocent manslayer to escape the vengeance of angry people.

The Lord also made arrangements for the nation to add three more cities of refuge if the borders of their land were expanded. He had promised Israel a large land (Gen. 15:18; Ex. 23:31), and if they had obeyed His law, He would have kept His promise. It was only during the reign of David that this much territory was actually held by Israel, and then they lost it when things fell apart during Solomon's reign.

—*Be Equipped*, page 152

8. Why did God direct the Israelites with such specific instructions about cities? How does that compare to the way we hear God today? In the Old Testament, God's provision and protection were often tied to the people's obedience. Is that still true today? Explain.

84

More to Consider: Murder was one of several capital crimes in Israel. Others were idolatry and sorcery (Lev. 20:1–6), blasphemy (24:10–16), violating the Sabbath (Num. 15:32–36), willful and repeated disobedience to parents (Deut. 21:18–21; Ex. 21:15, 17), kidnapping (v. 16), bestiality (22:19), homosexuality (Lev. 20:13), adultery (Deut. 22:22), and the rape of an engaged maiden (vv. 23–27). How does this list compare with capital crimes today? Why the notable differences?

From the Commentary

After Israel conquered the land of Canaan, each tribe was assigned its territory and their borders accurately described. Joshua, Eleazar the high priest, and the heads of the twelve tribes cast lots and made the assignments (Josh. 14:1–2). Within the tribes, each family and clan would make its own claim and mark it out with boundary stones. In that day, officials didn't draw detailed real estate maps, what we today call "plats." Everybody was expected to honor the landmarks (boundary stones), because to move the stones meant to steal land from your neighbors and their descendants (Prov. 22:28). Unscrupulous officials could easily exploit poor widows and orphans and take away their land and their income (15:25; 23:10–11). Since God owned the land and the people were His tenants, moving the stones also meant stealing from God, and He would punish them (Hos. 5:10). No wonder this crime was included among the curses announced from Mount Ebal (Deut. 27:17).

—*Be Equipped*, page 155

9. What is the overall message in the passage about the thief (Deut. 19:14)? What are the broader implications of the commandment "You shall not steal" (Ex. 20:15)? What, in addition to property, can be stolen by others? How do we continue to deal with this issue in today's world?

From the Commentary

The Jews weren't entering Canaan as sightseers but as soldiers prepared for battle and expecting God to give them victory. It's important to note that God gave the nation two different military approaches, one for the cities *in* the land of Canaan (Deut. 20:1–9, 16–18) and the other for cities *outside* Canaan (vv. 10–15). After Israel had conquered the land and was settled down in their inheritance, they might have to attack a distant city, because there were always enemies to deal with, and they could always accept the challenge of claiming God's promise and enlarging the land (19:8–9).

Moses didn't minimize either the size or the strength of the enemy, for he knew that the nations living in Canaan had horses, chariots, large armies, and fortified cities. The spies who had investigated the land thirty-eight years before had seen all these obstacles and dangers (Num. 13) but had failed to see how small these matters were when compared with the greatness of their God. Moses reminded the people that the Lord had successfully brought them from the land of Egypt to the plains of Moab and defeated every enemy that had attacked them. In fact, the territory Israel now inhabited belonged to the Jews and not to the enemy, because the Lord had given His people great victory over the nations east of the Jordan. Just as the Lord had defeated Pharaoh and his army in Egypt, so He would defeat the nations in Canaan.

—*Be Equipped*, pages 157–58

10. In the early days of the Great Depression, President Franklin D. Roosevelt said in his inaugural address, "The only thing we have to fear is fear itself." How was this true of the Israelites on the cusp of entering Canaan? How did Moses address that fear? Why did Israel actually have nothing to fear?

Looking Inward

Take a moment to reflect on all that you've explored thus far in this study of Deuteronomy 16:18—18:8; 19:1—21:14; 26:1–19. Review your notes and answers and think about how each of these things matters in your life today.

> *Tips for Small Groups: To get the most out of this section, form pairs or trios and have group members take turns answering these questions. Be honest and as open as you can in this discussion, but most of all, be encouraging and supportive of others. Be sensitive to those who are going through particularly difficult times and don't press for people to speak if they're uncomfortable doing so.*

11. Have you ever had a disagreement with a leader who had questionable character? How did that turn out? What role does a person's faith play in defining his or her character? How does your faith shape your character?

12. The Old Testament repeatedly reveals the dangerous tendencies of human nature (to seek pleasure above all else, pursue evil, etc.). What are areas of life where you struggle against your human nature? How does your relationship with God help you deal with those struggles?

13. What are some of the ways fear has kept you from doing what God is asking? What does this say about your faith? What are some practical ways to overcome that fear?

Going Forward

14. Think of one or two things that you have learned that you'd like to work on in the coming week. Remember that this is all about quality, not quantity. It's better to work on one specific area of life and do it well than to work on many and do poorly (or to be so overwhelmed that you simply don't try).

Do you want to address a worldly tendency and trust God's direction? Go back through Deuteronomy 16:18—18:8; 19:1—21:14; 26:1–19 and put a star next to the phrase or verse that is most encouraging to you. Consider memorizing this verse.

Real-Life Application Ideas: What does it mean for you to be a good citizen? How does that reflect your faith life? This week, spend time considering how you relate to others at home, work, and church. Are you honest? Generous? Are you being obedient to God in all your interactions with others? Do you recognize and honor God's goodness in your daily life? Be intentional in considering these aspects of being a godly citizen, and work on those areas where you find your behavior and attitudes lacking.

Seeking Help

15. Write a prayer below (or simply pray one in silence), inviting God to work on your mind and heart in those areas you've noted in the Going Forward section. Be honest about your desires and fears.

Notes for Small Groups:

- *Look for ways to put into practice the things you wrote in the Going Forward section. Talk with other group members about your ideas and commit to being accountable to one another.*

- *During the coming week, ask the Holy Spirit to continue to reveal truth to you from what you've read and studied.*

- *Before you start the next lesson, read Deuteronomy 21:15—25:19. For more in-depth lesson preparation, read chapter 9, "Disputes and Decisions," in* Be Equipped.

Disputes
(DEUTERONOMY 21:15—25:19)

Before you begin …
- *Pray for the Holy Spirit to reveal truth and wisdom as you go through this lesson.*
- *Read Deuteronomy 21:15—25:19. This lesson references chapter 9 in* Be Equipped. *It will be helpful for you to have your Bible and a copy of the commentary available as you work through this lesson.*

Getting Started

From the Commentary

The major emphasis in Deuteronomy 21:15—25:19 is on how the law of the Lord governed relationships in the nation of Israel. The material is so varied that perhaps the best way to study what Moses said is to arrange it in general categories.

The first category is protecting the family (21:15–21; 24:1–5; 25:5–10). The foundation for human society is the family, a gift from God for which no successful substitute has been found. Sociologist Margaret Mead said, "No matter how many communes anybody invents, the family keeps creeping back." It was God who established the home and in so doing remedied the only thing that was "not good" in His creation, that the man was alone (Gen. 1:26–31; 2:18–25). The people of Israel were commanded to honor father and mother (Ex. 20:12), and since four generations might live together as an extended family, that honor covered a lot of territory.

—*Be Equipped*, page 169

1. Family is a common theme in the Old Testament. Why is such emphasis placed on this particular theme? What does this reveal about the culture of the time? What does it reveal about God's character? How has this emphasis changed over time? Is that a good thing or a bad thing? Explain.

2. Choose one verse or phrase from Deuteronomy 21:15—25:19 that stands out to you. This could be something you're intrigued by, something that makes you uncomfortable, something that puzzles you, something that resonates with you, or just something you want to examine further. Write that here.

Going Deeper

From the Commentary

The original divine pattern for marriage was one man and one woman devoted to each other for one lifetime, and the two exceptions—polygamy and divorce—were permitted in Israel because of the "hardness of men's hearts" (Matt. 19:3–9). The first polygamist was Lamech, a rebel against God (Gen. 4:19), and the men in Scripture who followed his example brought heartache and trouble into their homes. Jacob discovered that having multiple wives meant competition and friction in the home and brought a great deal of grief into the family (Gen. 29:30; 31:1ff.). God overruled the selfishness in the home and accomplished His purposes in building the nation, but some of the family members paid a price.

At Passover, God spared the firstborn Jewish males who were sheltered by the blood of the lamb. In honor of this gracious miracle, He commanded that all the firstborn of Israel, man and beast, should be dedicated to Him (Ex. 13:1–16). Israel was God's firstborn son (4:22–23), and Israel's firstborn also belonged to Him. It was also ordained that the firstborn son in the family would inherit a double portion of the estate. If there were two sons, the elder son received two-thirds and the younger son one-third. Nothing could change this law, not even the husband's love for his favorite wife.

—*Be Equipped*, pages 169–70

3. Review Deuteronomy 21:15–17. Why was the firstborn son given special privilege? Didn't this mean that God was playing favorites? Why or why not? How did the gospel message change this particular law? Why is that important to us today?

More to Consider: In salvation history, it should be noted that God occasionally bypassed the firstborn son and chose the second born. Abraham's firstborn son was Ishmael, but God chose Isaac, and Esau was Isaac's firstborn, but God chose Jacob (Rom. 9:6–13). Jacob gave the special blessing to Ephraim, Joseph's second son, and not to Manasseh, the firstborn (Gen. 48). What does it say about God that He sometimes appears to go against the very laws He's set up? How does God teach through the unexpected?

From the Commentary

The rebellious son in Deuteronomy 21:18–21 was the original "prodigal son" (Luke 15:11–32), except that he didn't leave home to disobey the fifth commandment, dishonor his parents, and disgrace his community. Day

after day, he resisted the pleas, warnings, and chasten-
ings of his parents as he refused to work, reveled with the
drunkards, and contributed nothing to the home or the
community. This kind of sin was so heinous that it was
included in the curses read in the land of Canaan (Deut.
27:16; see Ex. 21:17).

This was more than a family concern, for it involved the
peace and reputation of the community.

—Be Equipped, pages 170–71

4. What was God's answer to the problem of the rebellious son? What does
this teach us about the importance given to reputation in Moses' time? Is
that still true today? What is an appropriate way to deal with a rebellious
child today?

From Today's World

The family in Moses' time was much different from the modern American
family. Today's family is diverse, scattered, broken, and often incomplete.
And rather than sharing a home with generations, today's family members
are often separated by thousands of miles. Our Internet-connected world

has in some ways been able to shrink those miles—people can communicate and even see each other on their laptops or phones—but the relationship between generations is still much different than it once was.

5. How has modern technology negatively affected the family? How has it positively affected the family? What are the biggest threats to the modern family? How can the modern family not only survive but also thrive in a world that is constantly changing and is rife with challenges to its integrity?

From the Commentary

It's bad enough when a family has a rebellious son to disturb the home, but it's even worse when the husband and wife don't get along and the marriage breaks up. The original Edenic law of marriage said nothing about divorce (Gen. 2:18–25). Marriage is fundamentally a physical union ("one flesh"), so only a physical reason can dissolve it, and there are two such reasons: the death of one spouse (Rom. 7:1–3; 1 Cor. 7:39) and adultery (Deut. 22:22; Lev. 20:10). The adulterous man and woman were killed, leaving the innocent spouses free to remarry. The law of Moses did not allow divorce for adultery because the guilty spouse was stoned to death for his or her sin.

Since the "uncleanness" ("something indecent," Deut. 24:1 NIV) couldn't be adultery, what was it that permitted a man to divorce his wife? In our Lord's day, the rabbinical school of Hillel took a very broad view and interpreted "uncleanness" to mean "anything that displeased the husband." But the school of Rabbi Shammai took the narrow view that "uncleanness" meant some kind of sexual sin. (See Matt. 5:31–32; 19:1–9; Mark 10:1–12.) Jesus didn't define "uncleanness" but made it clear that the Mosaic law of divorce was a concession and not a command. God permitted it because of the hardness of the human heart. However, it appears that Jesus did permit divorce if one of the spouses committed adultery. The assumption is that the innocent spouse was free to remarry; otherwise, why get a divorce?

—Be Equipped, page 172

6. Review Deuteronomy 24:1–4. What was God's overall message about divorce? Why would God permit divorce because of adultery? How does our modern world deal with these issues? What is the church's responsibility today in dealing with divorce? Who decides when divorce is permitted?

From the Commentary

The Lord used both positive and negative imagery to teach His people to respect and obey His law. On the positive side, the men wore blue tassels on the corners of their clothing to remind them that they belonged to the Lord and were privileged to have His law to obey (Num. 15:37–41). The weekly Sabbath and the annual feasts were reminders of all that the Lord had done for Israel, and the presence of God's sanctuary kept the Lord's presence before their eyes. The Levites scattered throughout Israel were living reminders of the law of the Lord and the importance of knowing it.

On the negative side, the offering of blood sacrifices was a vivid reminder that the basis of forgiveness and fellowship was the surrendering up of life (Lev. 17:11). Whenever the community stoned a lawbreaker to death, it would cause the people to "hear and fear." Isolating the lepers outside the camp, burning leprous garments, and tearing down leprosy-infested houses reminded the people that sin is like leprosy and must be dealt with. But the public exposure of a criminal's corpse would be an object lesson few would forget. A criminal found guilty of committing a capital crime was stoned to death, and if the officials wanted to make the judgment even more solemn, they could order the body hanged from a tree or impaled on a pole until sundown.

—*Be Equipped*, page 175

7. What was the purpose of "negative" lessons such as in Deuteronomy 21:22–23? Why wouldn't God always use positive examples to make His point? What does this teach us about God's character? Has any of this changed because of the gospel message? Explain.

From the Commentary

> Another category is loving one's neighbors (Deut. 22:1–4, 6–8; 23:24–25). These regulations are specific applications of Leviticus 19:18, "You shall not take vengeance, nor bear any grudge against the children of your people, but you shall love your neighbor as yourself: I am the LORD" (NKJV). The neighbor is a brother, which is even a greater motive for helping him, and God is the Lord of both, which is the highest motive of all. In fact, the Jews were to extend this same concern even to their enemies' animals (Ex. 23:4).
>
> —*Be Equipped*, page 176

8. Read Matthew 5:43–48 and Romans 12:17–21. What did Jesus and Paul have to say about loving our enemies? How does this commandment

work in concert with those that demand consequences for sin? How are loving your neighbor and loving your enemy related?

More to Consider: There were few fences and walls on Jewish farmland, so it would be easy for livestock to wander away. If you found such an animal, you were to return it to the rightful owner; if the owner lived too far away, you were to board the animal until the owner could come get it. Farm animals were both expensive and essential; neither the farm family nor the nation could survive without them. But Moses didn't limit the law to restoring just stray animals; he said that anything a Jewish person found was to be guarded and returned to the owner. A neighbor wasn't only the person who lived adjacent to you; a neighbor was anybody in need whom you could help (See Luke 10:25–37). How is this message about finding lost animals similar to Jesus' teaching about lost sinners (See Luke 15:1–7; James 5:19–20).

From the Commentary

The next category is maintaining distinctions (Deut. 22:5, 9–10). Because the Israelites were God's chosen people, separated from other nations, practices that were acceptable in pagan cultures were prohibited to the Jews. God set apart the priests and Levites to teach the people how to know right from wrong and the clean from the unclean, and this helped the people develop discernment. As they obeyed God and sought His blessing, they learned more and more of what was fitting and proper in Jewish society. The nation decayed spiritually because the priests and Levites failed to do their job, and the Jews began to imitate their heathen neighbors (Ezek. 22:23–29; 44:23).

The familiar and now accepted word "unisex" first appeared in print in *Life* magazine (June 21, 1968) in an article describing unisex clothing as "good fashion as well as good fun." In Deuteronomy 22:5, God calls it "an abomination." However, people who agree with Moses don't always agree with one another on how this law should be applied in the church. Since Christians aren't under the old covenant, some believers disregard the law completely, while others use it to tell the women in their churches how they should dress, both at home and in public. We can't ignore God's revelation in the Old Testament, because Jesus and the apostles used the Old Testament in their discussions of spiritual concerns. Even if this law about clothing doesn't apply to the church in the same way it applied to Israel, there are spiritual principles behind it that are important to us (2 Tim. 3:16–17).

—*Be Equipped*, pages 178–79

9. In what ways does the law in Deuteronomy 22:5 focus on more than clothing? What would our world look like if we applied this law strictly to believers today? Should we? Why or why not? What does this law (and others we've been studying) teach us about the role culture plays in our understanding of Scripture?

From the Commentary

> The final category is honoring personal purity (Deut. 22:13–30). "Sex has become one of the most discussed subjects of modern times," said Fulton J. Sheen. "The Victorians pretended it did not exist; the moderns pretend that nothing else exists." God created sex and has every right to control the way we use it, and if we obey Him, it will bring enrichment and enjoyment. One of the basic rules is that sex must not be experienced outside of the bonds of marriage.
>
> —*Be Equipped*, page 181

10. Why does the law of Moses speak so directly about a highly personal subject such as sexuality? Why is purity such an important theme in the

New Testament? What does this say about the greater purposes of purity? What does it say about the importance of honesty and loyalty in marriage?

Looking Inward

Take a moment to reflect on all that you've explored thus far in this study of Deuteronomy 21:15—25:19. Review your notes and answers and think about how each of these things matters in your life today.

> *Tips for Small Groups: To get the most out of this section, form pairs or trios and have group members take turns answering these questions. Be honest and as open as you can in this discussion, but most of all, be encouraging and supportive of others. Be sensitive to those who are going through particularly difficult times and don't press for people to speak if they're uncomfortable doing so.*

11. What value do you put on family? What are some ways (if any) that your family has helped you grow spiritually? What are some ways (if any) your faith has been inhibited or challenged by your family? Does the Bible's emphasis on the importance of family encourage you? Concern you? Explain.

12. The Old Testament is full of stories that describe the firstborn getting a better deal than the other siblings. Have you seen this in your own experience? If so, how did that make you feel? How important is fairness to you? How does that line up with the world in which you live? How does your relationship with God level the playing field?

13. What are some of the negative lessons that have affected your faith experience? What are some of the positive lessons? Which had the greater impact? How can both help you grow closer to Christ?

Going Forward

14. Think of one or two things that you have learned that you'd like to work on in the coming week. Remember that this is all about quality, not quantity. It's better to work on one specific area of life and do it well than

to work on many and do poorly (or to be so overwhelmed that you simply don't try).

Do you want to take a step to pursue purity in life? Be specific. Go back through Deuteronomy 21:15—25:19 and put a star next to the phrase or verse that is most encouraging to you. Consider memorizing this verse.

Real-Life Application Ideas: This week is all about family. Whether you're a parent, a grandparent, a sibling, or even an orphan—you have people you consider family. Take time this week to celebrate each member of that family in ways that honor each person's uniqueness. Take your sister out for ice cream. Build a fort for your son or daughter. Clean up that garage for your spouse. Don't make a big deal out of your actions—just do them and enjoy the God-given joy of being a part of a family.

Seeking Help

15. Write a prayer below (or simply pray one in silence), inviting God to work on your mind and heart in those areas you've noted in the Going Forward section. Be honest about your desires and fears.

Notes for Small Groups:

- *Look for ways to put into practice the things you wrote in the Going Forward section. Talk with other group members about your ideas and commit to being accountable to one another.*

- *During the coming week, ask the Holy Spirit to continue to reveal truth to you from what you've read and studied.*

- *Before you start the next lesson, read Deuteronomy 26:16—31:13. For more in-depth lesson preparation, read chapter 10, "Obedience and Disobedience, Blessings and Curses," in* Be Equipped.

Blessings and Curses
(DEUTERONOMY 26:16—31:13)

Before you begin ...
- *Pray for the Holy Spirit to reveal truth and wisdom as you go through this lesson.*
- *Read Deuteronomy 26:16—31:13. This lesson references chapter 10 in* Be Equipped. *It will be helpful for you to have your Bible and a copy of the commentary available as you work through this lesson.*

Getting Started
From the Commentary

In his brief introduction to this final section of Deuteronomy, Moses reminded the people that he had given them the Word of the Lord, the commandments of the true and living God (26:16–19). He also reminded them that at Sinai the nation had vowed to obey all that God said to them (Ex. 19:7–8; 24:3–8), and that the Lord had promised to bless them if they obeyed Him from the heart (Deut. 7:6–16). There on the plains of Moab, the Israelites would accept this solemn commitment a second time, and then they would affirm it a third time when they entered the Promised Land (Josh. 8:30–35). It isn't enough for God's people to enjoy the blessings and privileges of the covenant; they must also accept the responsibilities that are involved. Moses explained these responsibilities and called for the people to commit themselves wholly to the Lord.

—Be Equipped, pages 193–94

1. Once again Moses reminded the people of something they already should have known. Why does Scripture include a record of all this reminding? What does it teach us about human nature? About God's persistence?

2. Choose one verse or phrase from Deuteronomy 26:16—31:13 that stands out to you. This could be something you're intrigued by, something that makes you uncomfortable, something that puzzles you, something that resonates with you, or just something you want to examine further. Write that here.

More to Consider: Note in Deuteronomy 27 that Moses joined with the elders (v. 1) and the priests (v. 9) in announcing the covenant to the people. Moses would soon leave the scene, but the nation would continue and the Lord's authority would operate through their civil and religious leaders. What does this tell us about Moses? In what ways was he trying to divert focus from himself to the laws God had given him to share? What does this teach us about leadership?

Going Deeper

From the Commentary

As the spiritual leaders read the curses (Deut. 27:14–26), they weren't predicting what would happen if the people disobeyed God. They were calling upon the Lord to send these curses on His people if they turned away from Him. And when the people said "Amen" after each statement ("so be it"), they were telling God that they were willing to be chastened if they disobeyed Him. Their "Amen" wasn't just their agreement with the words spoken; it was their acceptance of the terms of the covenant. These curses were closely related to the law Moses had delivered and explained, especially the Ten Commandments.

The first curse (v. 15) condemned idolatry (Ex. 20:1–6). To carve or cast an idol and worship it was to deny that Jehovah was the one true and living God, and it was this sin that finally brought the wrath of God on Israel. Even if a Jew worshipped an idol in secret and didn't try to persuade anybody to join him, it was still a great sin and had to be punished (Deut. 13). The second curse related to the family and the home (27:16; Ex. 20:12), and the third to property (Deut. 27:17; 19:14; Ex. 20:15). The fourth curse (Deut. 27:18) revealed God's special concern for people with disabilities. Leviticus 19:14 mentions both the deaf and the blind.

—Be Equipped, page 195

3. Review Deuteronomy 27:14–26. Describe each of the first four curses. How does each of these relate to the commandments? How might the threat of a curse have influenced the people's choices?

From the Commentary

In the fifth curse (Deut. 27:19), the focus is on treating with kindness and justice the helpless and unfortunate in the land. Widows, orphans, and aliens were often abused and exploited in Israel and God called on His people to champion their cause and see that they received justice (24:17–18; Ex. 22:21–24; Luke 18:1–8). The Jews had been aliens in Egypt for many years and the Lord cared for them and judged the people who abused them. If Israel didn't care for the needy, God would also judge them. Among other things, this meant bringing their special tithes to the Lord every third year so the needy would have food to eat (Deut. 14:28–29).

Curses six through nine (27:20–23) have to do with sexual purity and relate to the seventh commandment (Ex. 20:14). These sins were prevalent among the nations in Canaan, and Israel wasn't to imitate their neighbors. Incest (Deut. 27:20, 22–23) was especially condemned in Israel (22:30; Lev. 18:8–9, 17; 20:11). Reuben lost his rights as the firstborn because he violated this law (Gen. 35:22; 49:3–4). Bestiality (Deut. 27:21; Lev. 18:23) was practiced in some pagan religions and "sacred animals" were used in the worship of their false gods. The perversion of sex is not only the abuse of a gift from God, but it threatens marriage and the family, which are foundational to the success of the nation.

The tenth and eleventh curses (Deut. 27:24–25) are an echo of the sixth commandment, "Thou shalt not kill" (Ex. 20:13). This command speaks of a deliberate deed (murder) and not accidental death (manslaughter; 21:12–14). Murder is the ultimate crime because its consequences can't be reversed, but to murder one's neighbor makes that crime even worse. The only thing more heinous would be to be paid to murder somebody! The law of Moses condemned those who accepted bribes to break the law, for making money is not more important than maintaining justice (Deut. 16:19; Ex. 23:8). The law taught the people of Israel to love their neighbors and do them good (Lev. 19:18; Deut. 22:1–4). But whether a neighbor or a total stranger is the victim, murder is wrong and murderers must be punished.

—Be Equipped, pages 195–96

4. Review the fifth through ninth curses (Deut. 27:19–23). How do we deal with these same themes in today's church? What wisdom can we take from each of these curses?

From Today's World

Churches today tend to respond to sinful behavior in one of two ways—by ignoring it or by offering grace without addressing the sin directly. For better or worse, the leadership in most church communities doesn't take people aside to address their sins and to offer guidance on how to turn away from them. When the church ignores blatant sin, at best it presents a message that suggests sin isn't so bad after all, and at worst it creates an environment in which people can be hurt by the actions of others. While offering grace is certainly biblical, when done alone, it can also cause problems by ignoring what otherwise could be damaging and dangerous behaviors.

5. Why does so much of the modern church seem hesitant to address sin directly? Are there ways to offer grace while also calling out sin? Explain. What is a biblical way to deal with someone who is engaged in sinful behavior? Whose responsibility is it to confront that behavior?

From the Commentary

> The twelfth curse (Deut. 27:26) obligated the Jews to obey every law that God gave them, whether it was named in this list or not. Paul quoted this verse in Galatians 3:10 to prove that there could be no salvation by obeying the law, since nobody could obey everything God commanded. But the purpose of the law was not salvation but condemnation, the indictment of all people as sinners, and therefore the need of all people to trust Christ, "for the just shall live by faith" (Gal. 3:11).
>
> —*Be Equipped*, pages 196–97

6. To say that we've kept some of God's laws doesn't excuse us, for to break one is to break them all (James 2:10–11). How does the twelfth curse (Deut. 27:26) speak to this issue? How does it speak to the issue of human nature? How does it indirectly address the idea of what it means to be holy?

From the Commentary

> God promised to bless His people in all places—the city,
> the field, and the home—with all that they needed. As
> they went in and out in their daily work (Deut. 28:6;
> 8:17–18), He would care for them and prosper their
> efforts. He would give them victory over their enemies
> so that they could maintain possession of the land. He
> would supply rain for the fields, for water is a precious
> commodity in the East. God would send the "former
> rain" in October and November, the "winter rain" from
> December to February, and the "latter rain" in April, and
> Israel's crops would grow abundantly. They would sell
> their surplus harvests to other nations but wouldn't have
> to buy from anybody.
>
> —*Be Equipped*, pages 197–98

7. Review Deuteronomy 28:1–14. Why do you think the Lord promised
these marvelous blessings? Why is obedience worthwhile even if it doesn't
bring material blessings? Besides blessings, what else does obedience bring?

From the Commentary

Deuteronomy 28:15–68 is predictive; it describes the judgments God promised to send on the nation if the people refused to obey His law.... God wanted His people to know that when these calamities struck, they would recognize the hand of the Lord and not think it was a series of coincidences.

Just as God promised to bless them in every area of life if they obeyed His covenant, so He warned that He would curse them in every area of life—their bodies, families, fields, flocks, and herds—if they disobeyed. They would be sick in body and mind, deprived of the necessities of life, defeated in battle, and scattered throughout the world. The word "destroyed" is repeated ominously (Deut. 28:20, 24, 45, 48, 51, 61, 63) as are the words "smite" and "smitten" (vv. 22, 25, 27–28, 35). The Jews would be consumed by disease and famine and defeated in war, with their dead bodies left unburied to become food for birds and animals. (For a body to be left unburied was a terrible disgrace for a Jew.) They would experience the diseases and plagues they saw in Egypt; they would see their wives ravished and their children slain before their eyes. Finally, they would go into captivity and serve their enemies. Then they would learn that serving God wasn't so difficult after all, but then it would be too late.

—*Be Equipped*, pages 198–99

8. In what ways are these judgments (Deut. 28:15–68) just the opposite of the blessings (vv. 1–14)? Why did the Jews at this point in history (just before entering the Promised Land) need to hear all these judgments? What did this say about their past behavior? About their relationship with God? How did Jesus' life, death, and resurrection change all that?

More to Consider: Many believe the "nation … from far away, from the ends of the earth" that will swoop down like the eagle (Deut. 28:49) is Babylon, but it could also refer to other nations. How important is it to know exactly what nation the eagle represents? What is the message, regardless of the specific interpretation?

From the Commentary

The word *covenant* is used seven times in Deuteronomy 29…. Moses reviewed the past (vv. 1–8), called the people to obey God's law (vv. 9–15), and warned them what would happen if they disobeyed (vv. 16–29). As we read and study Moses' farewell address, we may get weary of these repeated themes, but they are the essence of God's covenant with His people. While the priests and Levites had a copy of the law of Moses and could refer to it (17:18; 28:58; 29:20, 27; 31:26), the common people had to depend on their memories, and therefore repetition was important. "For me to write the same things to you is not tedious, but for you it is safe" (Phil. 3:1 NKJV). Too often God's people forget what they ought to remember and remember what they ought to forget!

—*Be Equipped*, page 202

9. Note all the uses of the word *covenant* in Deuteronomy 29. What is a covenant? How does the covenant declared in the chapter further explain and apply the covenant made at Mount Sinai?

From the Commentary

So often in Scripture, the thundering voice of judgment is followed by the loving voice of hope. Alas, Israel did forsake the Lord and follow after idols, and the Lord did bring on His people the judgments stated in His covenant. No nation in history has suffered as much as the nation of Israel, and yet no nation has given so much spiritual wealth to the world. In Deuteronomy 30, Moses looked down through the centuries and saw the future restoration of Israel in their land and under the blessings of God.

"Heart" is one of the key words in chapter 30 (vv. 2, 6, 10); the others are "command" or "commandment" (vv. 2, 8, 10, 11, 16), "turn" or "return" (vv. 2, 3, 8, 10), and "life" (vv. 15, 19, 20). The connection is obvious: If God's people turn from their sins and return with all their hearts to God and God's commandments and obey them, they will enjoy life as only the Lord can give. Moses is here looking forward to the time when a chastened Israel will repent, turn from their wicked ways, and come back to the Lord.

To some extent, a regathering occurred after the Babylonian captivity, when a believing remnant returned to the land and rebuilt the temple, but the fulfillment of this promise (vv. 3–6) will not take place until the end times. The people of Israel today are scattered throughout the world, while in the nation of Israel there are about six million people. But the Lord promises to regather His people, bring them back to their land, and bless them. But first, a spiritual "operation" must take place, the circumcision of their hearts so that they will receive their Messiah, love their Lord, and experience the spiritual life that He promised.

—*Be Equipped*, page 205

10. Review Deuteronomy 30. Bible scholars disagree about the future of Israel. Some say that the church is now "spiritual Israel" and that all of these Old Testament promises are now being fulfilled in a spiritual sense in the church. Others say that the Old Testament promises must be taken at face value and that we should expect a fulfillment of them when Jesus Christ returns to establish His kingdom on earth. Which perspective do you think is correct? Explain. How has this issue become a component in the discussion on the conflict in the Middle East? Why does this matter to modern-day Christians?

Looking Inward

Take a moment to reflect on all that you've explored thus far in this study of Deuteronomy 26:16—31:13. Review your notes and answers and think about how each of these things matters in your life today.

Tips for Small Groups: To get the most out of this section, form pairs or trios and have group members take turns answering these questions. Be honest and as open as you can in this discussion, but most of all, be encouraging and supportive of others. Be sensitive to those who are going through particularly difficult times and don't press for people to speak if they're uncomfortable doing so.

11. Moses had to remind the people over and over again about God's law. What are the aspects of living a life of faith that benefit from reminders? How can regular study of Scripture help you remember those things? What are other ways to remind yourself of what it means to be a Christ follower?

12. One of the lessons in this section of Deuteronomy is that breaking a single commandment or law can lead to breaking others. How have you seen this played out in your life? Why is it still important to follow God's commandments? What does it mean to follow those commandments out of love instead of obligation?

13. What does the covenant in the Old Testament mean to you? How do these curses and blessings impact your faith story? What are some of the Old Testament teachings that affect your daily expression of faith?

Going Forward

14. Think of one or two things that you have learned that you'd like to work on in the coming week. Remember that this is all about quality, not quantity. It's better to work on one specific area of life and do it well than to work on many and do poorly (or to be so overwhelmed that you simply don't try).

Do you want to be more conscious of the covenant God has made with His people, which includes you? Be specific. Go back through Deuteronomy 26:16—31:13 and put a star next to the phrase or verse that is most encouraging to you. Consider memorizing this verse.

Real-Life Application Ideas: The emphasis on curses and judgment in Deuteronomy can be daunting and depressing. But on the other side of those themes is blessing. This week, spend time being thankful for every blessing God has given you. Look for them in every aspect of your life—at home, at work, and among strangers and friends. There are evidences of God's blessing everywhere. Sometimes it just takes being intentional to see them.

Seeking Help

15. Write a prayer below (or simply pray one in silence), inviting God to work on your mind and heart in those areas you've noted in the Going Forward section. Be honest about your desires and fears.

Notes for Small Groups:

- *Look for ways to put into practice the things you wrote in the Going Forward section. Talk with other group members about your ideas and commit to being accountable to one another.*

- *During the coming week, ask the Holy Spirit to continue to reveal truth to you from what you've read and studied.*

- *Before you start the next lesson, read Deuteronomy 31:14—34:12. For more in-depth lesson preparation, read chapters 11 and 12, "The Song of Moses" and "The End of an Era," in* Be Equipped.

Moses' Song
(DEUTERONOMY 31:14—34:12)

Before you begin ...
- *Pray for the Holy Spirit to reveal truth and wisdom as you go through this lesson.*
- *Read Deuteronomy 31:14—34:12. This lesson references chapters 11 and 12 in* Be Equipped. *It will be helpful for you to have your Bible and a copy of the commentary available as you work through this lesson.*

Getting Started

From the Commentary

"These people will soon prostitute themselves to the foreign gods of the land they are entering" (Deut. 31:16 NIV).

That's the message the Lord gave Moses after he finished his farewell address to the people he had served so faithfully for forty years. Certainly these words grieved his heart, but Moses knew that Israel had a long history of turning away from the Lord and worshipping idols.

At Sinai they had made a golden calf and indulged in a pagan orgy (Ex. 32), and at Kadesh-barnea they wanted to appoint a new leader and return to Egypt (Num. 14). In both rebellions, it was the intercession of Moses that saved the nation from being destroyed by God's judgment. During their wilderness journey, the Jews had frequently complained to Moses about the way he was leading them. When the new generation arrived at the border of Canaan, the men indulged in immorality and idolatry with the women of Moab, and God sent a plague that killed 24,000 Israelites (Num. 25). Israel's history was a tragic story indeed.

—*Be Equipped*, page 211

1. What were some of the ways Moses encouraged his people to stay true to their Lord? How did the appointment of Joshua as his successor encourage the people? How did the book of law encourage them? What are some things your church leaders do to encourage you? How can you share those things with the people in your community?

More to Consider: Moses was eighty years old when God called him to lead His people (Ex. 7:7), and then he went on to serve the Lord and His people for forty years. Moses was still physically fit (Deut. 34:7), but the Lord had told him that, because of his sin at Kadesh, he wouldn't be allowed to enter Canaan (Deut. 1:37–38; 3:23–27; 4:21–22; Num. 20:1–13). Why would God deny Moses' entry into the Promised Land? What message did that send to the people?

2. Choose one verse or phrase from Deuteronomy 31:14—34:12 that stands out to you. This could be something you're intrigued by, something that makes you uncomfortable, something that puzzles you, something that resonates with you, or just something you want to examine further. Write that here.

Going Deeper

From the Commentary

In the work of the Lord, there's no substitute for godly leadership. As Moses did with Joshua, Christ with His apostles, and Paul with Timothy and Titus, the older generation must equip the younger generation to take their place (2 Tim. 2:2). The Lord has given us the qualifications for leaders in the church (1 Tim. 3; Titus 1), and we must give ourselves to mentoring and training qualified people to become those leaders. "The final test of a leader," wrote political columnist Walter Lippmann, "is that he leaves behind him in other men the conviction and the will to carry on." Leaders must not only be qualified, but they must also be prepared and proved (1 Tim. 3:10) so that they aren't novices in serving the Lord (v. 6). The absence of gifted and qualified leaders is sometimes evidence of God's judgment on His people (Isa. 3:1–4, 12; 57:1).

—*Be Equipped*, page 213

3. Review Deuteronomy 31:1–8, 23. Why was Joshua a worthy successor to Moses? How did the culture of the time determine who would be an acceptable leader? How are our leaders chosen today? What lessons can we take from this story to help us make good leadership choices in the church?

From the Commentary

At Mount Sinai, the Lord made it clear to Israel that, unlike the nations around them, they were to be a people of the word who would hear God's voice and obey it. The pagans could see their man-made idols but couldn't hear them speak, because their idols were dead (Ps. 115:1–8). If Israel forsook the living words of the living God and bowed down to dumb idols, they would be living by sight and not by faith and forsaking divine truth for human superstition. It was by the Word that the Lord created the universe, and it is through that same Word that He accomplishes His purposes in history (Ps. 33:6–13).

During his long ministry, Moses had kept a record of what God had done and said (Ex. 17:14; 24:4–8; 34:27; Num. 33:2; Deut. 28:58; 29:20, 27), and he deposited that record with the priests who carried the ark of the covenant. He commanded them to put the book beside the ark in the Holy of Holies, where He was enthroned on the mercy seat between the cherubim (Ps. 80:1 NIV). God rules His world through His Word and God's people must respect His Word and obey it. In future years, Israel's king was required to write a copy of the law, study it, and keep it with him (Deut. 17:18–20). Each Sabbath Year, at the Feast of Tabernacles, the law was to be read and expounded publicly to every man, woman, and child, whether Israelites or strangers, so that they would hear, fear, and obey (Neh. 8). It was especially important that the children hear the word (Deut. 31:13) so they could learn it early and enjoy a long life in the Promised Land.

Moses bluntly told the people what the Lord had told him: They were rebellious and stiff-necked and, after his death, would turn away from the Lord to worship idols (Deut. 31:27).

—*Be Equipped*, pages 213–14

4. Read Exodus 32:9; 33:3, 5; 34:9; Deuteronomy 9:6, 13; 10:16. What do these verses tell us about "stiff-necked" people? In what ways is hearing God's Word, meditating on it, and obeying it the best remedy against apostasy? What is the lesson in this for God's people today (See 1 Tim. 1:11, 18–19; 6:20; 2 Tim. 1:13–14; 2:2)?

From the Commentary

God instructed Moses to meet Him at the tabernacle and to bring Joshua, his successor, with him. Speaking from the glory cloud, the Lord told the two men that Israel would turn from the true and living God and worship idols ("play the harlot"), and that He would turn away from them and send the judgments named in the covenant (Deut. 28). The cause of their apostasy would be not only the pagan influence around them, but also their own prosperity in the land (31:20). They would forget God the generous Giver and cease to thank Him for His goodness. If the nation obeyed God and served Him joyfully, His face would shine upon them (Num. 6:22–27), but if they turned to idols, God would hide His face from His people and chasten them.

The Lord instructed Moses and Joshua to write down a song that He would give them, a song that the people could easily learn and remember. This song would warn the new generation and generations to come against the perils of idolatry and the tragic consequences of apostasy. It would also remind them of the goodness and mercy of the Lord. After Moses and Joshua wrote down the song (Deut. 31:19), they taught it to the leaders (v. 28) and to all the congregation (v. 30). Moses prefaced the song with the solemn reminder that, after his death, they would abandon the Lord and thereby invite the chastening of the Lord. This sounds something like Joshua's farewell speech to the officers and the people (Josh. 23—24), and Paul's last words to the Ephesian elders (Acts 20:17–37).

The song has four major divisions: the character of God (Deut. 32:1–4); the kindness of God to His people (vv. 5–14); the faithfulness of God to chasten His people (vv. 15–25); and the vengeance of God against His adversaries (vv. 26–43).

—*Be Equipped*, pages 216–17

5. Review Deuteronomy 31:14–22, 30; 32:1–43. What do each of the four sections noted in the previous commentary excerpt teach us about God's relationship with His people during Moses' time? How are these areas relevant to the church today?

From the Commentary

The "Song of Moses" had been a lesson in theology, history, and personal obedience, with several strong warnings included, but the final blessing Moses bestowed on his people is saturated with grace and mercy. It's quite a contrast to the "blessing" Jacob gave his sons before he died (Gen. 49), revealing their hidden character and exposing sin. Moses opened and closed his speech by extolling the greatness of the Lord he was about to meet on top of the mount (Deut. 33:1–5, 26–29), and then he named each tribe except Simeon and gave them a blessing from the Lord.

—*Be Equipped*, page 225

6. Why might Moses have written and spoken of himself in the third person in Deuteronomy 33:1, 4? (See David's similar approach in 2 Sam. 7:20.) What blessings did God give to the tribes in Deuteronomy 33? Why did Moses focus so much on blessings here? What did that reveal about Moses' heart? About God's heart for His people?

From the Commentary

> As Moses looked back over his long life, the one scene that gripped his mind was the revelation of God's glory at Mount Sinai (Ex. 19:16–25; 24:15–18; Heb. 12:18–21) and the giving of the law. But he had seen God's glory up close when he had been on the mount interceding with the Lord (Ex. 33—34). This same description is used in Deborah's song in Judges 5:4–5, and also by the prophet Habakkuk as he praised the Lord (Hab. 3:3). The better we know the Word of God, the more able we are to express proper worship to Him. There is no substitute for "psalms and hymns and spiritual songs" (Eph. 5:19; Col. 3:16) that are founded on Scripture.
>
> —*Be Equipped*, page 226

7. Why did God come from the myriad of angels in heaven to meet with sinful Israel (See Deut. 33:3)? What are some of the ways Moses emphasized God's love throughout the book of Deuteronomy (See 4:31–40; 7:6, 13; 14:2; 26:19; 28:9)? What should be our response to God's sovereign grace and love? What is our status with God today (See 2 Cor. 5:21)?

From the Commentary

> Deuteronomy 33:26–29 includes the last written words
> of Moses, and it focuses on the happiness of the people of
> God because of His blessings. As Moses finished blessing
> the tribes, he visualized the whole nation and the joy Israel
> ought to have because they know the true and living God.
> Their God isn't a dead idol sitting in a temple; He rides
> the heavens to come to the aid of His people (Ps. 18:10;
> 68:33)! But even more, God is Israel's "home" and dwell-
> ing place (see 90:1), and they abide in Him no matter
> where they go. As we go forward by faith, He defeats the
> Enemy and holds us up in the battle.
>
> —*Be Equipped*, pages 231–32

8. God gave the Israelites victory in many battles as they fought to take
the Promised Land. What then was their greatest danger? How would idol
worship once again trip them up? What was God's ultimate response to
their continued sin?

From the Commentary

The imminent death of Moses is a repeated theme in these closing chapters (Deut. 31:1–2, 14, 16, 26–29; 32:48–52; 33:1; 34:1–8, 10, 12). Moses knew what was coming, for death is an appointment (Heb. 9:27), not an accident. Moses had begun his ministry as a lonely shepherd, caring for his sheep near Horeb (Sinai), the mountain of God (Ex. 3), and now he would end his ministry, leaving his sheep with Joshua and going up Mount Nebo alone to meet God.

But the emphasis in these verses isn't so much his death as the fact that the Lord couldn't allow him to enter the Promised Land because of his rash sin at Kadesh (Num. 20). Instead of speaking to the rock, Moses struck the rock in anger and said, "Listen, you rebels, must we bring you water out of this rock?" (v. 10 NIV). His attitude, his actions (hitting the rock), and his words were all generated by the flesh and not the Spirit and were intended to glorify him and Aaron and not the Lord. Moses did not sanctify God in what he said and did, and for this he was kept out of the Promised Land (Deut. 1:37–40; Num. 20:12–13). He prayed earnestly that the Lord would change His mind, but the Lord refused to do so (Deut. 3:23–26; the verb indicates that Moses had often prayed this prayer).

—*Be Equipped*, pages 232–33

9. On Mount Nebo, Moses was perhaps six miles from the border of the Promised Land, but the Lord wouldn't allow him to enter it. Was the punishment greater than the offense? Explain. How might the story have played out differently if God had let Moses enter the Promised Land?

From the Commentary

> Moses was a meek man, and Jesus said, "I am meek and lowly in heart" (Matt. 11:28–30). Moses finished the work God gave him to do (Ex. 39:42–43; 40:33) and so did the Son of God (John 17:4). Before He returned to heaven, Jesus left trained disciples behind to continue the work of world evangelism, and Moses left Joshua and the elders behind to guide the people in the ways of the Lord. Our Lord's face shone on the Mount of Transfiguration, and Moses' face shone when he came down from meeting God on the mount (Matt. 17:2; Ex. 34:29–30). Moses was "mighty in words and in deeds" (Acts 7:22), and so was Jesus when He was ministering on earth (Luke 24:19).
>
> —*Be Equipped*, page 236

10. What are other ways that Moses reminds us of Jesus? How do his words and deeds encourage us to become more like our Savior?

Looking Inward

Take a moment to reflect on all that you've explored thus far in this study of Deuteronomy 31:14—34:12. Review your notes and answers and think about how each of these things matters in your life today.

Tips for Small Groups: To get the most out of this section, form pairs or trios and have group members take turns answering these questions. Be honest and as open as you can in this discussion, but most of all, be encouraging and supportive of others. Be sensitive to those who are going through particularly difficult times and don't press for people to speak if they're uncomfortable doing so.

11. What are some ways leaders have encouraged you in your faith? How is their encouragement important to your growth as a believer?

12. What do you think of when you hear the phrase "God's glory"? How have you experienced God's glory? What does it mean to you to glorify God?

13. Has God ever told you no in response to something you wanted to do? Describe that situation. What did it feel like to be told no? What did you learn from the experience?

Going Forward

14. Think of one or two things that you have learned that you'd like to work on in the coming week. Remember that this is all about quality, not quantity. It's better to work on one specific area of life and do it well than to work on many and do poorly (or to be so overwhelmed that you simply don't try).

Do you want to resist an idol in your life? Be specific. Go back through Deuteronomy 31:14—34:12 and put a star next to the phrase or verse that is most encouraging to you. Consider memorizing this verse.

Real-Life Application Ideas: The book of Deuteronomy is all about preparing and equipping God's people to enter the Promised Land. This week, consider the ways you're preparing and equipping yourself to live a life that's pleasing to God. Make a list of all the things you do to grow your faith, and spend time in prayer thanking God for all the ways He provides to equip you for this life and the next. Ask Him to show you how you can help equip others as well. Then be intentional in working on your faith development and on sharing with others what you know and discover.

Seeking Help

15. Write a prayer below (or simply pray one in silence), inviting God to work on your mind and heart in those areas you've noted in the Going Forward section. Be honest about your desires and fears.

Notes for Small Groups:

- *Look for ways to put into practice the things you wrote in the Going Forward section. Talk with other group members about your ideas and commit to being accountable to one another.*
- *During the coming week, ask the Holy Spirit to continue to reveal truth to you from what you've read and studied.*

Summary and Review

Notes for Small Groups: This session is a summary and review of this book. Because of that, it is shorter than the previous lessons. If you are using this in a small-group setting, consider combining this lesson with a time of fellowship or a shared meal.

Before you begin …
- *Pray for the Holy Spirit to reveal truth and wisdom as you go through this lesson.*
- *Briefly review the notes you made in the previous sessions. You will refer back to previous sections throughout this bonus lesson.*

Looking Back

1. Over the past eight lessons, you've examined Deuteronomy. What expectations did you bring to this study? In what ways were those expectations met?

2. What is the most significant personal discovery you've made from this study?

3. What surprised you most about Deuteronomy? What, if anything, troubled you?

Progress Report

4. Take a few moments to review the Going Forward sections of the previous lessons. How would you rate your progress for each of the things you chose to work on? What adjustments, if any, do you need to make to continue on the path toward spiritual maturity?

5. In what ways have you grown closer to Christ during this study? Take a moment to celebrate those things. Then think of areas where you feel you still need to grow and note those here. Make plans to revisit this study in a few weeks to review your growing faith.

Things to Pray About

6. Deuteronomy is a book about understanding and following God's law. As you reflect on this theme, consider how God's law for the Israelites can work in tandem with Jesus' teachings to grow your faith.

7. The messages in Deuteronomy include love, worship, blessings, trust, purity, honesty, and obedience. Spend time praying on each of these topics.

8. Whether you've been studying this in a small group or on your own, there are many other Christians working through the very same issues you discovered when examining Deuteronomy. Take time to pray for them, that God would reveal truth, that the Holy Spirit would guide you, and that each person might grow in spiritual maturity according to God's will.

A Blessing of Encouragement

Studying the Bible is one of the best ways to learn how to be more like Christ. Thanks for taking this step. In closing, let this blessing precede you and follow you into the next week while you continue to marinate in God's Word:

May God light your path to greater understanding as you review the truths found in Deuteronomy and consider how they can help you grow closer to Christ.